SCHRIFTENREIHE DES IMT 3

Schriftenreihe des Instituts für
Management und Tourismus

Herausgegeben von Christian Eilzer,
Bernd Eisenstein und Wolfgang Georg Arlt

Christian Eilzer,
Bernd Eisenstein,
Wolfgang Georg Arlt

National Parks and Tourism

Answers to a Global Question from
the International Competence Network
of Tourism Management (ICNT)

Martin Meidenbauer »

Christian Eilzer, Studium International Tourism Management (Master of Arts), BWL-Studium (Dipl.-Kfm. FH), Projekttätigkeit für die inspektour GmbH, von 2004 bis 2006 wissenschaftlicher Mitarbeiter im Studiengang International Tourism Management an der FH Westküste, ab 2006 an der Hochschule Mitarbeiter im Institut für Management und Tourismus.

Dr. Bernd Eisenstein, Dipl.-Kaufmann und Dipl.-Geograph, Dr. phil. (Universität Trier); zahlreiche Beratungs- und Gutachtertätigkeiten im Tourismus. Seit 1997 Professor für Tourismusmanagement, seit 2006 Leiter des Instituts für Management und Tourismus (IMT) der FH Westküste und Geschäftsführer der IMT GmbH.

Dr. Wolfgang Georg Arlt, Studium der Sinologie, Soziologie und Politologie an der FU Berlin (M.A. und Dr. rer.pol.), Studienaufenthalte an der Fu-Jen University Hsinchu/Taiwan und Chinese University of Hong Kong. Reiseveranstalter, Organisator von Messen und Ausstellungen, Consultant. Seit 2002 Professor für Tourismuswirtschaft, seit 2007 Studiengangsleiter International Tourism Management an der FH Westküste.

Die Deutsche Bibliothek verzeichnet diese Publikation in der Deutschen Nationalbibliografie; detaillierte bibliografische Daten sind im Internet über http://dnb.ddb.de abrufbar.

© 2008 Martin Meidenbauer Verlagsbuchhandlung, München

Printed in Germany

Gedruckt auf chlorfrei gebleichtem, säurefreiem und alterungsbeständigem Papier (ISO 9706)

ISBN 978-3-89975-140-6

Verlagsverzeichnis schickt gern:
Martin Meidenbauer Verlagsbuchhandlung
Erhardtstr. 8
D-80469 München

www.m-verlag.net

Foreword

National Parks and other conservation areas, especially in North America, Africa and Asia, are already very significant tourist attractions worldwide and important destinations for incoming and domestic tourism (cp Job/Harrer/Metzler/Hajizadeh-Alamdary 2005, 1). Frequently, positive effects such as economic development perspectives, or the systematic conservation of natural and cultural resources as valued capital of many regions, are coupled with tourist use. At the same time, tourism has destructive tendencies and if ecologically vulnerable areas are excessively encroached upon, tourism can permanently damage its own means of existence.

This conflict and further questions were central issues at the 1st International Tourism Conference at the University of Applied Sciences in Heide on 23 and 24 November 2007. At this conference scientists from colleges in China, Mexico, New Zealand, Norway, Russia and South Africa belonging to the International Competence Network of Tourism Management (ICNT) initiated by the Department of Tourism at the University of Applied Sciences in Heide met with representatives from the State Office for the Schleswig-Holstein Wadden Sea National Park, from the Institute of Management and Tourism (IMT), and specialists from the tourism sector to talk about "National Parks and Tourism" and to share knowledge and experience.

The lectures and discussions emphasized the significance of national parks and other conservation areas for tourism. National parks the world over are eminently suitable for tourist use and are important tourist destinations due to their unspoiled natural areas. Kruger National Park in South Africa, Tongariro National Park in New Zealand and Schleswig-Holstein Wadden Sea National Park are just some examples. It became evident however, that the label "National Park" was not often a determining factor for the success of these areas as tourist destinations. Many regions were tourist attractions before they were designated as conservation areas. Their nomination opens new opportunities for these areas or indeed sets limitations for tourist use.

The conference showed that although there are similar concepts, problems and future perspectives worldwide in terms of interaction between national parks and tourism, regional differences still play a role. While attempting to achieve conservation aims and at the same time guarantee tourist use, these regional peculiarities must be heeded. Differences appear for example in terms of organization and responsibility for the management of conservation areas, amenability, categorizing conservation areas and objectives or even as regards the reasons for visiting national parks which can differ according to the source market and the conservation areas themselves.

In this anthology, participants of the 1st International Tourism Conference shed light on different aspects of the topic "National Parks and Tourism". National challenges and points for action are identified in the contributions by Anja Maschewski (Institute of Management and Tourism at the University of Applied Sciences in Heide), Matthias Poeschel (Tourism-Marketing Saxony-Anhalt GmbH), Christiane Gätje and Maren Babinsky (State Office for the Schleswig-Holstein Wadden Sea National park) and Manuel Woltering (Institute for Geography, Julius-Maximilians-University Würzburg). Contributions by Michael Lück (Auckland University of Technology), Fleur Fallon (formerly of the Institute of Management and Tourism in Heide), Oscar Mario Ibarra Martínez und Alexander Oliver Scherer Leibold (Universidad Anáhuac, Mexico Norte) as well as Wolfgang Georg Arlt and Honggang Xu (Institute of Management and Tourism in Heide and Sun Yat-sen University, Guangzhou) focus on practical examples, courses of action and perspectives from different parts of the world.

The wide spectrum of the individual contributions provides an insight into the state of tourism in national parks and renders it possible to examine the topic from various global perspectives and to benefit from these perspectives in the course of one's own work.

June 2008

Ellen Böhling
Christian Eilzer

Inhaltsverzeichnis

Touristische Vermarktung Deutscher Nationalparke: Stand und Ausblick

Anja Maschewski

1. Einleitung

Die touristische Vermarktung von und in Nationalparken ist für Deutschland noch immer als zurückhaltend zu beschreiben. Zwar haben sich die deutschen Nationalparke unter dem Dach der „Nationalen Naturlandschaften" zu einer gemeinsamen Vermarktungsplattform zusammen geschlossen (vgl. www.europarc-deutschland.de), doch zeigt der Blick hinter die Kulissen, dass die Umsetzung professioneller Marketingmaßnahmen in den Nationalparken auf Destinationsebene noch sehr unterschiedlich weit fortgeschritten ist. Dabei ist längst durch zahlreiche Studien und positive Erfahrungen verschiedener Nationalparke belegt, dass es sich in vielerlei Hinsicht „auszahlt", wenn Tourismus und Naturschutz starke Kooperationen eingehen (siehe hierzu auch die folgenden Beiträge in diesem Tagungsband von Poeschel, M., Gätje, Ch./Babinsky, M. und Woltering, M.). Professionelles Entwicklungsmanagement in Nationalparkregionen und daraus hervorgehende Naturerlebnisangebote erhöhen nicht nur die Wertschöpfung aller am Produkt beteiligten Akteure in der Destination. Sie tragen gleichzeitig dazu bei, dass die Akzeptanz gegenüber dem Schutzauftrag der Nationalparke deutlich erhöht wird – bei Einheimischen und bei Gästen. Eine klare strategische Ausrichtung der Nationalparke und ihrer Regionen ist jedoch Voraussetzung, denn: „Großschutzgebiete (GSG) können einer Region zum Alleinstellungsmerkmal verhelfen. Es ist jedoch nicht so, dass GSG touristische Selbstläufer sind. Ebenso wie andere Attraktionen müssen sie als touristische Anziehungspunkte geführt werden. So verstanden gelten für GSG dieselben Regeln des touristischen Marktes wie für andere Attraktionen auch." (Job et al. 2005, 85) Vor diesem Hintergrund drängen sich verschiedene Fragen auf: Welches sind die Märkte, die von Nationalparken und ihren Destinationen beworben werden? Welche Ziele verfolgen Nationalparke heute? Wo stehen sie in ihren Kooperationen in und mit den touristischen Destinationen? Wer sind die Gäste von Morgen? Und:

Welche Erfolgsfaktoren sind entscheidend für die touristische Vermarktung?

2. Auftrag der Nationalparke

Nationalparke gehören in Deutschland zum nationalen Naturerbe. Ihre Ausweisung erfolgt durch die Bundesländer im Benehmen mit dem Bundesministerium für Umwelt, Naturschutz und Reaktorsicherheit und dem Bundesministerium für Verkehr, Bau- und Wohnungswesen (BNatSchG § 22, Abs. 1 und 4). Laut § 24 BNatSchG sind Nationalparke:

„(1) (...) rechtsverbindlich festgesetzte einheitlich zu schützende Gebiete, die
1. großräumig und von besonderer Eigenart sind,
2. in einem überwiegenden Teil ihres Gebiets die Voraussetzungen eines Naturschutzgebietes erfüllen und
3. sich in einem überwiegenden Teil ihres Gebietes in einem vom Menschen nicht oder wenig zu beeinflussenden Zustand befinden oder geeignet sind, sich in einen Zustand zu entwickeln oder entwickelt zu werden, der einen möglichst ungestörten Ablauf der Naturvorgänge in ihrer natürlichen Dynamik gewährleistet.
(2) Nationalparke haben zum Ziel, im überwiegenden Teil ihres Gebiets den möglichst ungestörten Ablauf der Naturvorgänge in ihrer natürlichen Dynamik zu gewährleisten. Soweit es der Schutzzweck erlaubt, sollen Nationalparke auch der wissenschaftlichen Umweltbeobachtung, der naturkundlichen Bildung und dem Naturerlebnis der Bevölkerung dienen.
(3) Die Länder stellen sicher, dass Nationalparke unter Berücksichtigung ihres besonderen Schutzzwecks sowie der durch die Großräumigkeit und Besiedlung gebotenen Ausnahmen wie Naturschutzgebiete geschützt werden."

Wirtschaftliche Nutzungen der natürlichen Ressourcen durch Land-, Forst-, Wasserwirtschaft, Jagd oder Fischerei sind folglich weitgehend auszuschließen bzw. nur unter strikten Vorgaben der Naturschutzbehörden möglich. In Deutschland sind derzeit 14 Gebiete als Nationalpark ausgewiesen, mit einer Gesamtfläche von 962.146 ha (siehe auch Abb. 1 und 2).

Abb. 1: Nationalparke in Deutschland[1]

---

[1] Quelle: Bundesamt für Naturschutz (BfN) (2007), http://bfn.de/0308_nlp.html

Anja Maschewski

Name	Gründungsjahr	Gesamtfläche (ha)	Vorrangig geschützte Lebensräume
Bayerischer Wald (BY)	1970	24.217	Buchen-Bergmischwälder mit Tanne, Hochlagen-Fichten-wälder, Moore, Bergbäche, Blockhalden, Alpine Fels-schuttfluren
Berchtesgaden (BY)	1978	20.804	Rasengesellschaften und Latschengebüsche, subalpine, montane und submontane Wälder, Almweiden, Seen
Schleswig-Holsteinisches Wattenmeer (SH)	1985	441.500 (davon ca. 97,7 % Wasserfläche)	Wattenmeerökosysteme, Salzwiesen des Vorlandes, Sandbänke und Dünen
Niedersächsisches Watten-meer (NS)	1986	277.708 (davon ca. 91,8 % Wasserfläche)	Wattenmeerökosysteme, Salzwiesen und Dünen der Ostfriesischen Inseln
Hamburgisches Watten-meer (HH)	1990	13.750 (davon 97,1 % Wasserfläche)	Wattenmeer im Mündungs-gebiet der Elbe mit starkem Gezeiten- und Brackwasser-einfluss
Jasmund (MV)	1990	3.003 (davon ca. 22 % Wasserfläche)	Buchenwälder auf Kreide-standorten, Moore, Kreide-steilküste, küstennahe Ostsee
Sächsische Schweiz (SA)	1990	9.350	Sandsteinfelsen, submontane wärme- und trockenheits-liebende Wälder, Schlucht- und Schattenhangwälder
Müritz-Nationalpark (MV)	1990	32.200	Kiefern- und Buchenwälder, Erlen- und Birkenbruch, Seen, Röhrichte, Moore
Vorpommersche Bodden-landschaft (MV)	1990	80.500 (davon 84 % Wasserfläche)	Boddengewässer, Salzwiesen, Dünen und Röhrichte, Kiefern- und Buchenwälder, Trocken-rasen
Unteres Odertal (BB)	1995	10.418	Flussauenlandschaft, Altarme- und wasser, Ried- & Röhricht-bestände, Feuchtgrünland, Hangwälder, Steppenrasen

Hainich (TI)	1997	7.513	Laubmisch- und Buchen-wälder mittlerer und reicherer Standorte in unterschiedlichen Sukzessionsphasen
Eifel (NW)	2004	10.700	Atlantisch geprägte, boden-saure Buchenmischwälder (kollin bis submontan), Fich-tenforste, Magerwiesen, Fel-sen, Urft-Stausee
Kellerwald-Edersee (HE)	2004	5.724	Submontane, bodensaure Buchenwälder, felsig-trockene Steilhänge, Waldwiesen

Abb. 2: Informationen zu Nationalparken in Deutschland[2]

Für die internationale Anerkennung ist es für Nationalparke von beson-derer Bedeutung, von der internationalen Naturschutzorganisation IUCN als Nationalpark anerkannt zu werden. Diese hat ein international geltendes Klassifikationssystem für Schutzgebiete verfasst, das sechs Ka-tegorien ausdifferenziert, von denen eine für Nationalparke gilt (Katego-rie II) (vgl. EUROPARC und IUCN 2000). Die Einordnung eines Ge-bietes erfolgt darin nach den vorrangigen Managementzielen, die man mit den Schutzgebieten erreichen will. Nach den Richtlinien der IUCN lautet die Definition der Managementkategorie II (Nationalparke):

„Natürliches Landgebiet oder marines Gebiet, das ausgewiesen wurde um (a) die ökologische Unversehrtheit eines oder mehrerer Ökosysteme im Interesse der heu-tigen und kommenden Generationen zu schützen, um (b) Nutzungen oder Inan-spruchnahme, die den Zielen der Ausweisung abträglich sind, auszuschließen und um (c) eine Basis zu schaffen für geistig-seelische Erfahrungen sowie Forschungs-, Bildungs-, Erholungsangebote für Besucher zu schaffen. Sie alle müssen umwelt- und kulturverträglich sein." (EUROPARC und IUCN 2000, 13).

Prioritäre Managementziele von Nationalparken sind nach den Richtli-nien der IUCN Naturschutz sowie Tourismus und Erholung. So heißt es in den Managementzielen für Nationalparke: „Schutz natürlicher Regio-nen und landschaftlich reizvoller Gebiete von nationaler und internatio-naler Bedeutung für geistige, wissenschaftliche, erzieherische, touristi-sche oder Erholungszwecke; (...) Besucherlenkung für geistig-seelische,

---

[2] Quelle: http://www.bfn.de/0308_nlp.html, 14.05.2008

13

erzieherische, kulturelle und Erholungszwecke dergestalt, dass das Gebiet in einem natürlichen oder beinahe natürlichen Zustand erhalten wird;" Erläuternd wird hinzu gefügt: „Erholung gründet sich in diesen Gebieten zu allererst und vor allen Dingen auf Begegnung mit und Erleben von unberührter Natur."

Umwelt- und Naturbildung als Teil des Programms für Besuchermanagement und Erholung bilden eine vorrangige Aufgabe des Schutzgebietsmanagements. Förderung von Umweltbildung und Naturverstehen wird deshalb als zusätzliches Managementziel hervorgehoben (EURO-PARC und IUCN 2000, 24).

12 der 14 bestehenden Deutschen Nationalparke sind seit 2003 international als Nationalparke der IUCN-Kategorie eingestuft – nur die beiden Nationalparke Kellerwald-Edersee und Eifel entsprechen der IUCN Kategorie V (Geschützte Landschaft/Geschütztes Marines Gebiet) (vgl. Job et al. 2005, 16).

3. Touristische Nachfrage und Bildungsauftrag

Mit rund 20 Millionen Besuchern in den Deutschen Nationalparken wird ein touristischer Jahresumsatz von 0,3 Milliarden Euro erwirtschaftet (vgl. DTV 2005, 3). Im Jahr 2000 konnten bereits 48 Millionen Übernachtungen im Umfeld der damals 13 Nationalparke verzeichnet werden (Eifel Tourismus GmbH 2004). Diese Zahlen machen deutlich, dass Nationalparke auch für das Umfeld, dem sie angehören, eine hohe touristische Relevanz haben. Die wirtschaftliche Bedeutung der Nationalparke für den Tourismus ist heute unbestritten.

In Destinationen mit Nationalparken treffen naturschützerische und touristische Interessen unmittelbar aufeinander. Nationalparke haben neben dem Schutzauftrag einen Bildungsauftrag. Sie sollen Angebote für Umweltbildung und Naturerlebnis bereitstellen. Tourismus kann ihnen behilflich sein, diesen Bildungsauftrag zu erfüllen, denn der Trend zum Naturerlebnis und die Sehnsucht nach „intakter Natur" sind ungebrochen bei den deutschen Reisenden: 37 % der Befragten im Rahmen der Reiseanalyse 2005 nennen „Natur erleben, Landschaft, reine Luft" als wichtiges Urlaubsmotiv (F.U.R 2005), mit steigender Tendenz.

Bereits 1998 wurde in einer Studie des EMNID-Institutes im Auftrag des WWF (World Wide Fund of Nature) abgefragt, welche Bedeutung speziell Nationalparke für den Tourismus haben. Danach gaben 72 % der Bundesbevölkerung an, dass sie bevorzugt dort ihren Urlaub verbringen, wo man sich für den Schutz der Natur durch einen Nationalpark entschieden hat. Auch, wenn Reiseentscheidungen durch weitaus mehr Faktoren innerhalb eines komplexen Entscheidungsgefüges beeinflusst werden, ist dieses Ergebnis ein wichtiger Hinweis für alle Schutzgebiete: Nationalparke stehen für ein glaubwürdiges Prädikat, das für Umweltqualität und ein besonderes Naturerlebnis steht. Nationalparke sind zu Markenzeichen für eine intakte Naturlandschaft geworden, „(…) eine Eigenschaft, die zu den bedeutendsten Wettbewerbsfaktoren im Tourismus zählt." (Job et al. 2005, 16).

In Verbindung mit dem regionalen touristischen Angebot haben Nationalparke damit die Chance, ihr Natur- und Umweltverständnis einer breiten Öffentlichkeit zu kommunizieren und dadurch gleichzeitig für eine höhere Akzeptanz ihres Schutzauftrages zu sorgen. Umgekehrt sichert der Naturschutz die wichtigen landschaftsbezogenen Grundlagen für den Tourismus. Nationalparke sind überzeugende Image- und Werbeträger für die Vermarktung der gesamten Destination. „Die Vermarktung des Nationalparks macht diesen also zum Besuchermagneten, und erst durch die hohe Besucherfrequenz kann der Nationalpark seinen Bildungsauftrag erfüllen." (AUbE e.V. 2003, 13). Aber: Nutzen die Deutschen Nationalparke dieses Potenzial auch? Sind die Nationalparke eingestellt auf ihre Gäste? Welche zielgruppenspezifischen Angebote gibt es? Ein Blick in die aktuellen Ergebnisse einer Website-Analyse des Instituts für Management und Tourismus an der Fachhochschule Westküste lassen ahnen, welche Entwicklungsmöglichkeiten sich auch heute noch für Nationalparke eröffnen, wenn sowohl Zielgruppenansprache als auch die Verknüpfung mit dem touristischen Potenzial der Regionen von den Nationalparken als Chance für die eigene Attraktivierung begriffen wird (vgl. FHW 2008).

4. Nationalparke und touristische Vermarktung

4.1 Erfolgsfaktor Besuchermonitoring

In der touristischen Vermarktung von Destinationen stellen Nationalparke Teilelemente eines touristischen Gesamtangebotes dar. Bevor der
Gast den Nationalpark auch als touristisches Angebot wahr nimmt, be-
darf es einer touristischen „Inwertsetzung". Professionell konzipierte
Erlebnisangebote orientieren sich konsequent an den Wünschen der
Kunden. Voraussetzung dafür ist, dass man sich schon vor der eigentli-
chen Angebotsentwicklung ein detailliertes Bild über die vorhandenen
und potenziellen Kunden macht, um „maßgeschneiderte Antworten" auf
die Nachfrage zu geben: Welche Motivationen, welche individuellen Bedürfnisse bestimmen die Reisegewohnheiten des Gastes? Welches An-
forderungsprofil bringt er mit? Was veranlasst ihn in die Region zu reisen und: Welche Faktoren machen den Besuch des Nationalparks für ihn
– ganz individuell – attraktiv?

Die touristische Trend- und Motivforschung gibt zwar wichtige Hinweise für den Besucherrahmen, kann jedoch nicht die individuellen Gästebefragungen und regionsspezifischen Entwicklungskonzepte von Na-
tionalparkdestination ersetzen. So unterschiedlich wie die naturräumliche
und touristische Ausstattung der Regionen ist, die Lage und Historie etc.,
so heterogen ist auch die Gästestruktur der Nationalparkregionen. Die
Gäste der Wattenmeerregion sind beispielsweise durchschnittlich sehr
viel jünger als die der Mittelgebirgsregionen, was unmittelbar Einfluss
auf die Nachfragebedürfnisse hat (vgl. Eifel Tourismus GmbH 2004).
Eine kontinuierliche touristische Marktforschung ist daher unersetzlich.
„Gästebefragungen sind ein wichtiges, wenn nicht das wichtigste An-
wendungsfeld der touristischen Marktforschung. Die Einzigartigkeit von
touristischen Regionen macht es notwendig – will man Informationen
über die anwesenden Gäste und deren individuelle Reisegewohnheiten
haben – gezielte Befragungen durchzuführen. Nur auf diesem Weg ist es
möglich, ein regionen-/destinationsspezifisches Gästeprofil zu erstellen
(...)" (Freyer 1999).

In den Nationalparken ist die Besucher bezogene Datenerhebung bislang noch sehr lückenhaft. Zwar führen die meisten Nationalparke ein
Ökosystemmonitoring durch, ein Besuchermonitoring wird jedoch nur
von einigen wenigen umgesetzt. Für die gezielte Bewerbung touristischen Gästepotenzials ist dieses jedoch unerlässlich. Darüber hinaus lie-

fern die Erkenntnisse der Befragungen die Möglichkeit, die Effizienz von Besucherlenkung und -information zu kontrollieren. Als positives Beispiel sei hier das Sozio-ökonomische Monitoring (SÖM) der Wattenmeerregion genannt, in dem die Gästebefragung eines von drei Grundlagenmodulen der umfangreichen Marktforschung darstellt (vgl. auch den folgenden Fachbeitrag von Gätje, Ch./ Babinsky, M. in diesem Tagungsband). Die Ergebnisse der Gästebefragung sollten zu ihrer Umsetzung in einer klaren Entwicklungsstrategie für den Nationalpark münden, die als Maßnahmenpaket in ein Entwicklungskonzept und/oder den Nationalparkplan integriert werden. Best Practice Beispiele für Entwicklungskonzepte finden sich u.a. im Nationalpark Berchtesgaden (www.nationalpark-berchtesgaden.de) und im Nationalpark Eifel (www.nationalpark-eifel.de).

4.2 Erfolgsfaktor Zielgruppen-Kenntnis

Die Analyse der Websites der Deutschen Nationalparke zeigt deutlich, dass eine Zielgruppenansprache durch die Nationalparke gegenwärtig am konsequentesten für die Zielgruppen Kinder, Familien und Schulen umgesetzt ist (vgl. FHW 2008). Neun der 14 Deutschen Nationalparke halten spezielle Angebote für diese Besuchergruppen vor (vgl. Abb. 3). Ebenso viele haben ihre Nationalparke mit ansprechenden Ausstattungselementen für Kinder und Familien erlebbar gemacht: Speziell aufbereitete Lernmaterialien, Workshops und Exkursionen für Schülergruppen, spezielle Aktionstage, thematische Wanderrouten für Kinder, verknüpft mit Märchen und Erlebnispfaden, Forschungsstationen, Wildnis-Spielplätzen, Umweltbildungshäusern etc. stellen nur eine kleine Auswahl des vielseitigen Angebotes dar, das die Nationalparke ihren Gästen bieten (ebenda 2008).

Auch die Zielgruppe Jugendliche wird von fast 50 % der Deutschen Nationalparke gezielt angesprochen: Die Möglichkeit als Junior-Ranger im Nationalpark aktiv zu werden, Praktika zu machen oder an speziellen Aktionen in Jugendcamps teilzunehmen sind bewährte Angebote, mit denen Jugendliche an die Arbeit und die Schutzziele der Nationalparke heran geführt werden. Oft gibt es jedoch keine klare Altersabgrenzung zwischen den Angeboten für Kinder, Schüler und Jugendliche, so dass es für Besucher schwierig ist, ein wirklich passendes Angebot für den Nationalparkbesuch zu finden. Eine Datenmaske, die detaillierte Angaben

17

und Wünsche des potenziellen Gastes bereits im Eingang abfragt, ist nicht nur im Sinne des Besuchers kundenfreundlich, sondern gleichzeitig eine wertvolle Hilfe für die eigene Strukturierung der Angebote. Ein positives Beispiel gibt hier der Nationalpark Sächsische Schweiz, auf dessen Internetseite bereits alle Angebote nach Altersgruppen sortiert sind und entsprechend abgefragt werden können (www.nationalpark-saechsische-schweiz.de).

Besonders hervorzuheben sind ebenfalls die speziell gestalteten Kinderseiten von vier Nationalparken, die den Kindern auch im Internet einen besonderen, eigenen Zugang zur Nationalpark-Thematik ermöglichen: Die „Wattwurmbande" auf der Seite des Nationalpark Niedersächsisches Wattenmeer, die „Abenteuer Nationalpark-Seite" des Nationalpark Eifel, der Internetauftritt des Nationalpark Harz mit dem „Löwenzahn-Entdeckerpfad" sowie die Extra-Seiten des Nationalpark Berchtesgaden zeigen ansprechende Kommunikationspfade, in der die Nationalparkthemen nicht nur für Kinder interessant aufbereitet sind (vgl. FHW 2008).

Insgesamt ist festzuhalten, dass die gezielte Ansprache von Kindern, Familien und Schülergruppen auch aus touristischer Sicht unbedingt fortgeführt werden sollte bzw. dort entwickelt werden sollte, wo sie noch nicht selbstverständlicher Bestandteil des Nationalparkkonzeptes ist. Zahlreiche Best Practice Beispiele aus den Deutschen Nationalparken bieten bereits Orientierung und Ideen zum Nachmachen, wie in der folgenden Übersicht beispielhaft dargestellt (vgl. Abb. 3).

Kriterien	Anzahl Websites / von 14 Nationalparks	Best Practice Beispiele (Auswahl, u.a.)
Spezielle Angebote für Kinder (Ausstattung)	9	www.nationalpark-hainich.de (Baumkronenpfad)
Spezielle Angebote für Kinder (Veranstaltungen, Aktivitäten)	9	www.wattenmeer-nationalpark.de (Hallig-Schul-/Ausstellungsprojekt)
Spezielle Seite(n) im Internet für Kinder	4	www.nationalpark-eifel.de (Nationalpark Kinderseite mit Forschungsseite u.v.m.)

Spezielle Angebote für Jugendliche (Ausstattung)	6	www.nationalpark-eifel.de Wildnis-Werkstatt und Wildnis-Trail
Spezielle Angebote für Jugendliche (Veranstaltungen, Aktivitäten)	6	www.nationalpark-bayerischer-wald.de (Internationales Jugendlager)
Spezielle Angebote für ältere Reisende (Veranstaltungen, „Kombi-Aktivitäten")	2	www.wattenmeer-nationalpark.de (buchbare Kombipakete „Nationalpark-erlebnis")
Spezielle Angebote für ältere Reisende (Ausstattung, z.B. barrierefrei)	3	www.nationalpark-hainich.de (Barrierefrei ausgebauter Rundweg)
Spezielle Angebote für Best Ager (Veranstaltungen)	2	www.nationalpark-eifel.de (Kutschfahrten durch den NP)
Barrierefreie Führungen in die Landschaft	5	www.nationalpark-eifel.de (Führungen auch für Gehörlose mit Gebärdensprache etc.)
Spezielle Angebote für Schülergruppen	8	www.nationalpark-berchtesgaden.de (umfangreiches, vielseitiges Angebot)
Spezielle Angebote für Erwachsenengruppen	5	www.nationalpark-saechsische-schweiz.de (Veranstaltungen nach Altersgruppen in Datenmaske abrufbar)

Abb. 3: Zielgruppen spezifische Ansprache auf den Websites Deutscher Nationalparke 2008[3]

So positiv die Vermarktungsaktivitäten und -entwicklungen der meisten Nationalparke für die Zielgruppe Familien, Kinder und Jugendliche zu bewerten sind, so gering scheint die Kenntnis einiger Nationalparke über andere Zielmärkte zu sein, glaubt man den im Internet dargestellten Angeboten.

Besonders auffallend ist, dass das Potenzial der Zielgruppe der sogenannten „Best Ager" für die Vermarktung der Nationalparke bislang

---

[3] Quelle: FHW 2008

kaum genutzt wird. Nur zwei der 14 Deutschen Nationalparke halten derzeit Angebote bereit, in denen eine spezielle Kenntnis der Bedürfnisse älterer Reisender erkennbar ist. Mehrtagesangebote, beispielsweise kombiniert mit kulturtouristischen Angeboten der Region oder speziellen Tagesangeboten, in denen das Naturerlebnis bewusst mit dem Besuch einer ansprechenden Gastronomie verknüpft wird, finden sich nur punktuell auf den Seiten der Nationalparke (vgl. FHW 2008). Dabei ist längst bekannt, dass das Interesse an Naturerlebnissen mit zunehmendem Alter steigt (vgl. Studienkreis für Tourismus und Entwicklung in: DTV 2005, 7) Die Möglichkeit zum Naturerleben wird ab einem Alter von 30 Jahren sogar zu einem wichtigen Kriterium für die Auswahl des Reiseziels. Je nach Altersgruppe liegen die Werte hier sogar zwischen 54 und 60 %. Bei den Unter-Dreißigjährigen spielt das Naturerleben dagegen eine geringere Rolle (ebenda 2005).

Vor dem Hintergrund des demografischen Wandels ist zukünftig sogar von einer noch stärker wachsenden Anzahl Natur interessierter Reisender auszugehen. Schon heute hat der Wunsch nach „Natur erleben" bei der Zielgruppe der sogenannten „Best Ager" einen sehr viel höheren Stellenwert als bei der durchschnittlichen Gesamtbevölkerung: Er rangiert auf Platz Zwei der „Top 10" der Urlaubsmotive, gleich hinter dem Motiv „Frische Kraft sammeln, Auftanken" (vgl. F.U.R 2007). Der Bedeutung der Zielgruppe „Best Ager" sollte daher mit einer starken Entwicklung von Angeboten und Aktivitäten begegnet werden, die den Ansprüchen dieser Gästegruppe gerecht wird.

Die gegenwärtigen Vermarktungsaktivitäten vieler Nationalparke beschränken sich meist auf das Angebot von Wander- und Radrouten sowie daran gekoppelte Veranstaltungen und Führungen. Zwar gehören Radfahren und Wandern zweifellos zu den beliebtesten Aktivitäten der Zielgruppe „Best Ager", sie werden im Urlaub jedoch vorzugsweise in Kombination mit anderen Erlebnissen wahrgenommen. Dem B.A.T. Freizeit-Forschungsinstitut zufolge lassen sich für die „Best Ager" drei Hauptmotive benennen, die für sie von großer Bedeutung sind und ihre Destinationswahl beeinflussen: 1. Natur, 2. Wellness und 3. Kultur. Die Reise erfahrenen 60+ legen weiterhin großen Wert auf Entspannung, Erholung, Komfort und Bequemlichkeit, Sicherheit und Verlässlichkeit. Bevorzugte Unterkünfte sind Hotels und Gasthöfe. Der Besuch einer Veranstaltung, die Besichtigung eines kulturellen Highlights sowie die Verknüpfung der Aktivität mit einem Besuch in der Gastronomie sind nur einige der möglichen Angebote, die kombiniert mit dem Aufenthalt in der Natur gerne vorzugsweise von Best Agern gebucht werden. Die besondere Herausforderung für die Nationalparke besteht darin, einen attraktiven Zusatznutzen für die Gäste zu schaffen, der das Wander- und/oder Radfahrerlebnis deutlich von dem anderer Regionen und Mitbewerber abhebt. Besondere Beachtung sollte dabei dem Bereich Service- und Produktqualität geschenkt werden, denn die demografische Entwicklung in Deutschland bedeutet nicht nur weniger Gäste, sondern insbesondere auch immer mehr Reise erfahrene Gäste. Die mittlerweile selbstbewusste touristische Nachfrage macht immer höhere Qualitätsansprüche geltend. Anpassungen der strategischen Ausrichtung, der Marketingaktivitäten (Innen- und Außenmarketing) und nicht zuletzt der Angebotsstrukturen werden notwendig. Ohne die enge Kooperation der Nationalparke mit den touristischen Destinationen, denen sie angehören, ist den Ansprüchen heutiger und zukünftiger Gästegruppen jedoch kaum noch gerecht zu werden.

4.3 Erfolgsfaktor Regionale Angebotsverknüpfung

Die wenigsten Gäste reisen allein wegen des Nationalparks in die Regionen. Laut Reiseanalyse waren „lediglich 7 Prozent bzw. 4,6 Millionen aller Urlaubsreisen im Jahre 2004 aus Sicht der Reisenden in erster Linie Naturlaube. Weitere 16 % der Reisen waren ‚unter anderem' Natururlauber. Bei ihnen war das Erleben der Natur nur einer von mehreren Urlaubsschwerpunkten" (RA 2005 in: DTV 2005, 7) Eine Besucherbefragung des Nationalparks Eifel bestätigt diese Ergebnisse deutlich. Danach nehmen die Gäste des Nationalparks Eifel den Nationalpark und seine angrenzenden Kommunen eindeutig als „räumliche Erlebniseinheit" wahr. Zahlreiche Aktivitäten der Nationalparkbesucher finden im weiteren Umfeld des Nationalparks statt (vgl. RWTH 2007).

Vor dem Hintergrund dieser Erkenntnisse erstaunt das Ergebnis der Website-Analyse der FHW (vgl. Abb. 4): Vertraut man den Aussagen der Internetseiten der Nationalparke, nutzt bislang lediglich die Hälfte der Nationalparke das regionale Potenzial zur Attraktivierung ihres eigenen Angebotes! Buchbare Angebote für Mehrtagesangebote finden sich gegenwärtig nur auf zwei der 14 betrachteten Internetauftritte. Sieben Nationalparke bieten ihren Besuchern Vorschläge für Mehrstunden- und/oder Tagesaufenthalte auf ihren Internetseiten, lediglich zwei stellen die tourismusrelevanten Einrichtungen der Region auf einer Karte dar. Immerhin 11 Nationalparke sind direkt mit den regionalen und lokalen Tourismusorganisationen und/oder -Informationen verlinkt, neun geben direkte Hinweise zu Beherbergungsmöglichkeiten in der Region und fünf weisen auf gastronomische Betriebe hin, die während des Aufenthaltes besucht werden können. Insgesamt zeigt das Ergebnis der Internetanalyse jedoch anhand weniger Kriterien, welche großen Entwicklungspotenziale bislang noch in der Vermarktung Nationalparke selbst liegen (vgl. Abb. 4). Der Verknüpfung mit regionalen Angeboten zur Attraktivierung des eigenen Angebotes kommt neben der konsequenten Zielgruppenorientierung eine zentrale Aufgabe innerhalb der Vermarktung von Nationalparken zu (vgl. FHW 2008). Ein gut gepflegtes Netzwerk an Kooperationspartnern, der kontinuierliche Informationsaustausch und die Kooperation bei der Angebotsentwicklung und Vermarktung sind die Grundvoraussetzungen für eine erfolgreiche Verknüpfung mit der touristischen Destination.

Als Best Practice Beispiel für die regionale Vermarktung und Kooperation sei hier der Nationalpark Jasmund genannt (www.koenigsstuhl.com), für den es seit September 2007 einen kommunalen Nationalparkrat gibt, kurz „KONRAT" genannt. Der Rat setzt sich aus Vertretern wichtiger Institutionen der Nationalparkregion sowie verschiedener Fach-Institutionen aus Landes- und Bundesebene zusammen. Gemeinsam trägt KONRAT dafür Sorge, dass der Leitgedanke des Nationalparks weiter von einer Mehrheit getragen wird. Die Vermarktung auf der Internetseite ist vorbildlich und zeigt die positiven Effekte eines funktionierenden Kooperationsmodells für alle im Nationalpark relevanten Aufgabenbereiche.

Auch auf der Internetseite des Nationalparks Sächsische Schweiz (www.nationalpark-saechsische-schweiz.de) findet sich ein gelungenes Beispiel für die Kommunikation des gesamttouristischen Potenzials in Verbindung mit dem Internetauftritt des Nationalparks. Der Gast erhält bereits auf der ersten Seite zahlreiche Hinweise auf mögliche Aktivitäten und interessante Themen der Destination. Neben den Informationen zur Landschaft finden sich auf gleicher Ebene Informationen zum Kunst- und Kulturraum Sächsische Schweiz. Zahlreiche Angebote und Verknüpfungen der Themen, beispielsweise über den Malerweg, eine interaktive Karte mit Tipps zu den Sehenswürdigkeiten etc. machen den Auftritt für die gesamte Destination attraktiv. Insbesondere für Urlaubsgäste mit dem Wunsch nach einem längeren Aufenthalt ist eine solche Darstellung von großer Bedeutung, aber auch Tagesgäste sind dankbar für einen schnellen Überblick und den leichten Informationsfluss.

Auswahl abgefragter Kriterien	Anzahl Websites / von 14 Nationalparks
Slogan für den Nationalpark	9
Gesamttouristische regionale Angebotspalette sichtbar	7
Karte der Region mit touristischen Informationen	2
Informationen zur Anreise mit dem PKW	5
Informationen zur Anreise mit Bus und/oder Bahn	8
Hinweis auf Sehenswertes der Region	6
Hinweis auf Aktivitätsmöglichkeiten	8
Interaktive Karte	5
Aktuelle, hervorgehobene Veranstaltungsinformationen	8
Hinweise zum regionalen gastronomischen Angebot	5
Informationen zu Unterkünften	9
Vorschläge für Tagesaufenthalt	7
Vorschläge für Mehrtagesaufenthalte	2
Informationen zu barrierefreiem Zugang touristischer Einrichtungen	2
Verlinkung zu Touristinformationen	11
Innovative Ideen/Angebote für das Nationalparkerlebnis	4
Prospekt-Zusendung und/oder Downloads	6

Abb. 4: Touristische Informationen auf den Websites Deutscher Nationalparks 2008[4]

---

[4] Quelle: FHW 2008

Im gesamten Ranking der touristischen Bewertung der Internetauftritte der Deutschen Nationalparke liegen der Nationalpark Eifel und der Nationalpark Jasmund mit ihren Websites weit vorne, gefolgt von dem Internetauftritt des Nationalparks Sächsische Schweiz und dem Nationalpark Hainich (vgl. FHW 2008).

5. Fazit

Naturschutz und Tourismus haben noch immer ein ambivalentes Verhältnis zueinander. Auch nach vielen Jahren gemeinsamer Arbeit, zahlreicher Studien, erfolgreicher gemeinsamer Entwicklungsprozesse etc. zeigt sich, dass noch ein großes Entwicklungspotenzial im Bereich der Produktentwicklung und Vermarktung vorhanden ist, das von vielen Nationalparken noch weitestgehend ungenutzt ist.

Ist das natürliche Potenzial einer Region aus touristischer Sicht – neben dem kulturellen Angebot – das wichtigste, was Destinationen zur Verfügung haben, um ihr Alleinstellungsmerkmal herauszuarbeiten und sich damit innerhalb des Gesamtmarktes klar zu positionieren; steht aus naturschutzfachlicher Sicht nach wie vor die Gefahr der Beeinträchtigungen durch Tourismus im Vordergrund: Ausbau der Infrastruktur, erhöhtes Verkehrsaufkommen, intensive Nutzung der Naturräume durch Aktivitäten der Gäste etc. Dabei ist längst durch zahlreiche Studien belegt, dass das Ausmaß ökologischer Beeinträchtigungen insbesondere von der Durchführung von Besucherlenkungsmaßnahmen abhängig ist, denn erst der ungelenkte Massentourismus stellt für die meisten Schutzgebiete eine Bedrohung ihrer Schutzaufträge dar. Richtig eingesetzt, kann auch die touristische Vermarktung Teil der Besucherlenkung werden, wie die zahlreichen guten Beispiele einiger Deutscher Nationalparke zeigen. Das Potenzial ist jedoch längst noch nicht ausgeschöpft, auch das ist deutlich geworden. Vor dem Hintergrund der im Wandel begriffenen Märkte, müssen Nationalparke zukünftig noch stärker als bisher die Angebote ihrer touristischen Regionen nutzen, um den Gästen von Morgen ein stimmiges Gesamtangebot zu präsentieren. Nur so ist langfristig auch gewährleistet, dass die Nationalparke ihrem Schutzauftrag und Bildungsauftrag gerecht werden können.

Literaturverzeichnis

AUbE (Akademie für Umweltforschung und -bildung in Europa e.V.) (Hrsg.) (2003): *Nationalparke als Wirtschaftsfaktor für eine nachhaltige Regionalentwicklung. Ergebnisse der Befragung der Nationalparke in Deutschland und Erwartungen für einen potenziellen Nationalpark Senne.* Rügen.

BfN (Bundesamt für Naturschutz) (2007): *Nationalparke.* http://bfn.de/0308_nlp.html.

DTV (Deutscher Tourismusverband e.V.) (2001): *Touristische Angebotsgruppe „Deutsche Nationalparke", Endbericht.* Bonn.

DTV (Deutscher Tourismusverband e.V.) (2005): *Natur. Erlebnis. Angebote. Entwicklung und Vermarktung, Leitfaden.* Bonn.

Eifel Tourismus GmbH (2004): *Touristischer Masterplan Erlebnisregion Nationalpark Eifel.* Aachen. S. 13.

EUROPARC und IUCN (The World Conservation Union) (2000): *Richtlinien für Managementkategorien von Schutzgebieten – Interpretation und Anwendung der Management Kategorien in Europa.* EUROPARC und WCPA. Grafenau. Deutschland. S. 24.

FHW (Fachhochschule Westküste), Institut für Management und Tourismus (IMT), Maschewski, A. (2008): *Website-Analyse zur touristischen Vermarktung Deutscher Nationalparke 2008.* Heide.

F.U.R (Forschungsgemeinschaft Urlaub und Reisen e.V.) (2005): *Kurzfassung Reiseanalyse 2005.* Kiel.

Freyer, W. (1999): *Tourismus-Marketing: marktorientiertes Management im Mikro- und Makrobereich der Tourismuswirtschaft.* München/Wien.

Job, H./Harrer, B./Metzler, D./Hajizadeh-Alamdary, D. (2005): *Ökonomische Effekte von Großschutzgebieten. Untersuchung der Bedeutung von Großschutzgebieten für den Tourismus und die wirtschaftliche Entwicklung von Regionen (= BfN-Skripten 135).* Bonn-Bad Godesberg.

Landesamt für den Nationalpark Schleswig-Holsteinisches Wattenmeer (Hrsg.) (2003): *Basisdokumentation Naturerlebnis Wattenmeerregion Eiderstedt/Dithmarschen.* Tönning.

Umweltrecht (2008): *Beck-Texte Umweltrecht (UmwR), 19. Auflage 2008.* DTV-Verlag.

RWTH (2007): *Besucherbefragung im Nationalpark Eifel und seiner angrenzenden Region 2007. Analyse und Vergleich mit der Analyse 2005. Bericht.* Aachen.

Internetseiten der Deutschen Nationalparke

www.nationalpark-bayerischer-wald.de
www.nationalpark-berchtesgaden.de
www.nationalpark-eifel.de
www.nationalpark-hainich.de
www.nationalpark-hamburgisches-wattenmeer.de
www.nationalpark-harz.de
www.nationalpark-jasmund.de
www.nationalpark-kellerwald-edersee.de
www.nationalpark-mueritz.de
www.nationalpark-wattenmeer.niedersachsen.de
www.nationalpark-saechsische-schweiz.de
www.nationalpark-wattenmeer.de
www.nationalpark-unteres-odertal.de
www.nationalpark-vorpommersche-boddenlandschaft.de
www.koenigsstuhl.com

Weitere Internetseiten mit Informationen zum Thema Nationalparke und Tourismus

www.bfn.de
www.deutschland-tourismus.de
www.dbu.de
www.europarc-deutschland.de
www.fahrtziel-natur.de
www.iucn.org
www.lustaufnatur.net
www.nabu-akademie.de
www.nationalparke.de
www.nationale-naturlandschaften.de
www.schoenste-parks.de
www.viabono.de
www.wwf.de
www.wanderbares-deutschland.de

Naturreich Sachsen-Anhalt:
Touristische Inwertsetzung von Großschutzgebieten

Matthias Poeschel

1. Mittendrin in Deutschland: Viele Wege führen nach Sachsen-Anhalt

Sachsen-Anhalt, zwischen Harz und Elbe, der Altmark im Norden und dem Burgenland im Süden, ist die Mitte Deutschlands und das achtgrößte Bundesland. Es ist umgeben von Brandenburg, Sachsen, Thüringen und Niedersachen. Das Land hat einiges zu bieten: ein wildromantisches Mittelgebirge, urtümliche Flusslandschaften und das sanfte Hügelland im Weinbaugebiet an Saale und Unstrut.

Auf dem Gebiet des heutigen Sachsen-Anhalt sind das älteste bekannte Sonnenobservatorium der Welt bei Goseck oder die bronzezeitliche Himmelsscheibe von Nebra Zeugnisse der hohen Entwicklung der menschlichen Gesellschaft im prähistorischen Europa. Im Mittelalter entwickelten sich im Schnittpunkt der Handelsstraßen bedeutsame Städte, wurden Waren, aber auch Gedanken ausgetauscht. So ist es wohl kein Zufall, dass auf dem heutigen sachsen-anhaltischen Gebiet so manche Geschichte ihren Ursprung hat. Otto der Große, der erste Kaiser des Heiligen Römischen Reiches Deutscher Nation, legte hier den Grundstock für sein mächtiges Imperium. Eine ganze Reihe weiterer wichtiger Ereignisse, Personen und historischer Prozesse haben hier ihre Wurzeln und wirken noch immer weit über die Landesgrenzen hinaus. Nur ein Beispiel dafür ist die Reformation. Martin Luther und Philipp Melanchthon, beide Professoren an der Universität in Wittenberg, haben mit ihrem Schaffen die Glaubenslandschaft in Deutschland und letztendlich weltweit nachhaltig verändert. Nicht umsonst wird Sachsen-Anhalt – das Kernland deutscher Geschichte – als „Land der Frühaufsteher" bezeichnet.[1]

Die naturräumlichen Gegebenheiten, der geschichtliche Hintergrund, die Innovationsfähigkeit der Menschen und eine zukunftsorientierte Inf-

---

[1] „Wir stehen früher auf." – Standortkampagne Sachsen-Anhalt, www.sachsen-anhalt.de/LPSA/index.php?id=Standortkampagne, 17.02.2008

rastruktur sind das Fundament, auf dem die Wirtschaft und der Tourismus in Sachsen-Anhalt bauen können.

2. Tourismus in Sachsen-Anhalt[2]

Der Tourismus ist für Sachsen-Anhalt ein immer mehr an Bedeutung gewinnender Wirtschafts- und Imagefaktor. Zentraler Ansatz für die erfolgreiche touristische Vermarktung des Landes ist eine Kombination aus Themen- und Destinationsmarketing. Die Profilierung und positive Imageprägung erfolgt in erster Line anhand der vertriebsorientierten Vermarktung der vier touristischen Markensäulen des Landes (s.u.). Unterstützend werden Schwerpunktthemen und Regionen kommuniziert.

Die Produktentwicklung richtet sich dementsprechend nach der Landesmarketingstrategie[3], die dynamisch ausgerichtet ist und gemäß den Marktanforderungen weiterentwickelt wird. Sachsen-Anhalt verfolgt dabei den integrativen Ansatz des modularen Produktaufbaus von kultur- und naturtouristischen sowie aktiv- und gesundheitsorientierten Angeboten. Das entspricht den Trends und Megatrends im Deutschlandtourismus und somit den aktuellen Ansprüchen des „multioptionalen Gastes".

Mit den vier touristischen Markensäulen „Straße der Romanik", „Gartenträume – Historische Parks in Sachsen-Anhalt", dem „Blauen Band – Aktivtourismus in Sachsen-Anhalt" und der Archäologieroute „Himmelswege" sowie den Schwerpunktthemen „UNESCO – Welterbe" und „Luthers Land" sowie „Musik" verfügt Sachsen-Anhalt über hervorragende Voraussetzungen zur Vernetzung der definierten touristischen Trends.

Die Markensäulen und Schwerpunktthemen werden in verschiedener Gewichtung in den vier Tourismusregionen des Landes: dem Harz, dem Gartenreich Dessau-Wörlitz/Anhalt-Wittenberg, der Weinregion Saale-Unstrut und der Altmark widergespiegelt.

---

[2] Ministerium für Wirtschaft und Arbeit des Landes Sachsen-Anhalt, Handbuch Tourismus in Sachsen-Anhalt, 2005
[3] Landesmarketing Sachsen-Anhalt GmbH, MASTERPLAN TOURISMUS – Handlungsstrategie 2004-2008, 2004

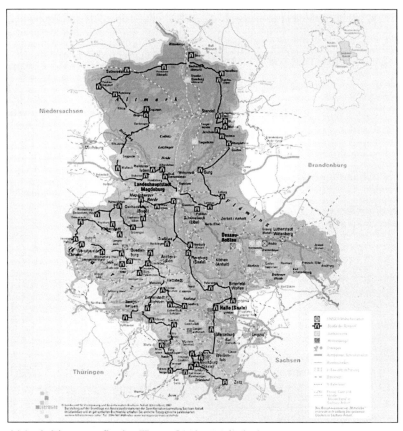

Abb. 1: Topografische Karte Sachsen-Anhalt[4]

Die Stellung, die Sachsen-Anhalt als Kernland deutscher Geschichte und einzigartige Kulturdestination innehat, ist unbestritten und wird durch die positive Entwicklung der touristischen Ankünfte und Übernachtungen in den letzten Jahren bestätigt.[5]

---

[4] Landesamt für Vermessung und Geoinformation Sachsen-Anhalt 2007
[5] Zwischen 2001-2006 steigen die Übernachtungszahlen um 624.339. Statistisches Landesamt Sachsen-Anhalt Halle (Saale), www.statistik.sachsen-anhalt.de/Internet /Home/Daten_und_Fakten/4/45/455/45511/Beherbergungen_Jahresangaben. html, 12.02.2008

Im Jahr 2007 verzeichnete Sachsen-Anhalt insgesamt 2,6 Millionen touristische Ankünfte. Zudem werden erstmals mehr als 6,5 Millionen Übernachtungen gezählt.[6] Mit diesem positiven Ergebnis bei den Übernachtungen ist Sachsen-Anhalt im prozentualen Vergleich der deutschen Bundesländer das erfolgreichste Flächenland Deutschlands. Die durchschnittliche Aufenthaltsdauer der Gäste von rund 2,5 Tagen in Sachsen-Anhalt spiegelt dabei den allgemeinen Trend zur Kurzreise in Deutschland wider.[7]

3. Touristisches Marketing in Sachsen-Anhalt

3.1 Die Landesmarketing Sachsen-Anhalt GmbH (1999 – 2006)[8]

Für mehr als sieben Jahre war die *Landesmarketing Sachsen-Anhalt GmbH (LMG)* für das strategische und operative touristische Außenmarketing des Reiselandes Sachsen-Anhalt federführend. Die Verantwortung für das Standortmarketing wurde der LMG im Jahr 2003 übertragen.

Zielsetzung im touristischen Außenmarketing war die Förderung privater, kommunaler und regionaler touristischer Leistungsträger vor Ort sowie die verstärkte Positionierung Sachsen-Anhalts im Wettbewerb der Länder im Deutschlandtourismus.

Die Basis für erfolgreiche Kommunikation und effektiven Vertrieb des touristischen Produktportfolios sind markt- und zielgruppengerechte, zukunftsfähige sowie wirtschaftlich tragfähige Angebote. Die dazu nötigen, gemäß der Marktanforderung qualitativ hochwertigen Pauschalen, Bausteine und weiteren Leistungen wurden von den touristischen Akteuren – in Zusammenarbeit mit den regionalen Fachverbänden, dem Landestourismusverband und der LMG – entwickelt. Damit wurde sowohl Reiseveranstaltern als auch Endkunden im Rahmen von klar nach-

---

[6] Ankünfte, Übernachtungen und Aufenthaltsdauer der Gäste in Beherbergungsbetrieben (einschließlich Camping)

[7] Statistisches Landesamt Sachsen-Anhalt Halle (Saale), Ankünfte und Übernachtungen im Reiseverkehr Monatsdaten für das Berichtsjahr 2007, www.stala.sachsen-anhalt.de/Internet/Home/Veroeffentlichungen/Pressemitteilungen/2008/03/36.html, 11.06.2008

[8] Landesmarketing Sachsen-Anhalt GmbH 2004, S. 21 ff

fragegetriebenen Vertriebs- und Kommunikationsaktivitäten die touristische Vielfalt des Reiselandes Sachsen-Anhalt erfolgreich offeriert.
Ende 2006 erfolgte eine strukturelle Neuausrichtung im Standort-
und damit auch im touristischen Marketing des Landes (s.u.). Erklärtes
Ziel bleibt es, den Anteil des Landes bei den relevanten Kennziffern im
Deutschlandtourismus nachhaltig zu erhöhen. Die Zahl der Ankünfte,
und der Übernachtungen in Sachsen-Anhalt soll weiter erhöht, die Ver-
weildauer möglichst verlängert und damit die Auslastung der Häuser
verbessert werden.

3.2   2007 – Neuausrichtung des touristischen Marketings: die Tourismus-Marketing Sachsen-Anhalt GmbH[9] und die Investitions- und Marketinggesellschaft Sachsen-Anhalt mbH[10]

Mit dem 1. Januar 2007 hat die *Tourismus-Marketing Sachsen-Anhalt GmbH
(TMG)* ihre Arbeit als Nachfolgerin der LMG aufgenommen. Ihre Bildung geht auf Beschlüsse der sachsen-anhaltischen Landesregierung zu-
rück, die darauf abzielen, der Tourismuswirtschaft die Möglichkeit zu
geben, sich an der GmbH direkt zu beteiligen und dadurch den Einsatz
öffentlicher Mittel für das Tourismusmarketing zu reduzieren.

Neben der TMG hat die – als Nachfolgerin der Wirtschaftsförderge-
sellschaft des Landes (WiSA) – neu gebildete Investitions- und Marketinggesellschaft Sachsen-Anhalt mbH (IMG) jene Teile des Tourismus-
marketings übernommen, die vor allem auf Image- und Standortentwick-
lung abzielen. So soll gewährleistet sein, dass künftig das gesamte Portfolio des sachsen-anhaltischen Angebots auch weiterhin am Markt angeboten wird.

Bei der TMG stehen Maßnahmen der Entwicklung, der Qualitätssi-
cherung, des Marketings und des Vertriebs touristischer Produkte im
Vordergrund. Die Gesellschaft bietet darüber hinaus weiterführende
Dienstleistungen für touristische Partner an. Die Gesellschaft ist stark

---

[9] Tourismus-Marketing Sachsen-Anhalt GmbH, www.sachsen-anhalt-tourismus.de
- TMG intern, 12.02.2008

[10] Investitions- und Marketinggesellschaft Sachsen-Anhalt mbH, www.img-sachsen-
anhalt.de, 12.02.2008

vertriebs- und verkaufsorientiert, sie besetzt dabei vor allem die folgenden Geschäftsfelder:

- Neue Medien, Internet, e-commerce
- Printprodukte für die Verkaufsförderung
- Messen, Präsentationen, Roadshows
- Kooperation mit Reiseveranstaltern und Reisebüros
- Beratung und Dienstleistungen für Dritte

Der Tourismuswirtschaft bietet sich die Chance, durch den Erwerb von
Gesellschafteranteilen unmittelbar Einfluss auf die Geschäftspolitik zu
nehmen. Andererseits wird die TMG auch allen anderen touristischen
und dem Tourismus nahe stehenden Partnern Möglichkeiten zum Anschluss und die Teilnahme an gemeinsamen Projekten anbieten.

Die *Investitions- und Marketinggesellschaft Sachsen-Anhalt mbH (IMG)*
zeichnet für alle Leistungen rund um die Förderung der Ansiedlung neu-
er Unternehmen verantwortlich. Durch Beratung und Betreuung ansäs-
siger Unternehmen verfolgt die IMG zudem das Ziel, den wirtschaftlichen Einfluss des Landes Sachsen-Anhalt deutschland-, europa- und
weltweit zu verbessern. Darüber hinaus ist die IMG für das Image- und
Standortmarketing sowie Teile des touristischen Außenmarketings Sachsen-Anhalts im In- und Ausland verantwortlich. Im Bereich Standortmarketing wird die Weiterführung der 2005 gestarteten überregional be-
achteten Image-Kampagne „Wir stehen früher auf!" koordiniert.

In ihrem touristischen Zweig unterstützt die IMG die dynamische
Fortschreibung der Landestourismusstrategie, dabei werden auf der
Grundlage fundierter Marktforschung Handlungsempfehlungen für mit-
tel- und langfristige Konzepte erarbeitet.

Die IMG ist federführend bei der Entwicklung und Umsetzung Erfolg
versprechender Vermarktungsthemen. Darüber hinaus werden die re-
nommierten Markensäulen „Straße der Romanik", „Blaues Band – Aktivtourismus in Sachsen-Anhalt", „Gartenträume – Historische Parks in
Sachsen-Anhalt" und die Archäologieroute „Himmelswege" (seit Mai
2008 die vierte Markensäule Sachsen-Anhalts) sowie die touristischen
Schwerpunktthemen weiterentwickelt. Über Fachbeiräte werden touristi-

sche sowie tourismusaffine Partner intensiv in das operative und strategische Tourismus-Marketing der IMG beratend eingebunden.[11]

TMG und IMG arbeiten koordiniert zusammen und setzen weiter darauf, das kultur- und das naturtouristische Potenzial des Landes Sachsen-Anhalt nachhaltig zu bewerben.

Besonders die von der LMG 2005 begonnenen Maßnahmen im Bereich der Vermarktung von Großschutzgebieten im Projekt „Naturreich Sachsen-Anhalt" werden aufgrund ihres Modellcharakters für den Deutschlandtourismus von IMG und TMG durch umfangreiche Marktanalysen qualifiziert und auf hohem Niveau fortgeführt.[12]

4. Die Nationalen Naturlandschaften und die Trends in Deutschlandtourismus

4.1 Die touristischen Trends in Deutschland: Kultur, Natur, Aktiv und Gesund

Innerhalb der touristischen Zielgruppen sind neue Gewichtungen zu erkennen. Eine Vernetzung von kultur-, natur-, aktiv- und gesundheitsorientierten touristischen Angeboten bietet neue Chancen. Dabei hat eine Destination zu entscheiden, in welcher Form das touristische Marketing zu erfolgen hat und ob eine Kombination von konzentriertem Themenmarketing mit einem zielgruppenspezifischen Marketing korrespondiert. Beispielsweise kann beim Wandern die Natur als Thema und die zahlungskräftige Zielgruppe der „Best Ager" im Mittelpunkt stehen.

Den differenzierten Motiven des „multioptionalen Gastes" wird schwerpunktmäßig besondere Aufmerksamkeit geschenkt:

- In Zeiten der Globalisierung und begünstigt durch Billigflieger spielt die Entfernung bei der Reisezielentscheidung eine untergeordnete Rolle. Jedoch ist, womöglich als Folge der Klimadiskussion, ein klarer Aufschwung im Deutschlandtourismus zu erkennen.
- Es wird heute kürzer, dafür häufiger und besonders außerhalb der Saison gereist. Die aktuelle Kampagne der Deutschen Zentrale für Tourismus (DZT) „Kurz-Nah-Weg" bedient diesen Trend z.B.

---

[11] IMG, www.img-sachsen-anhalt.de/?cid=119009000156, 12.02.2008
[12] Kap. 5 ff. e.d.

mit Städtereisen, Aktiv & Natururlaub bis hin zum gesundheitsorientierten Kurzurlaub in Deutschland.[13]

- Die Dynamik der Neuen Medien ermöglicht es, schnell und unkompliziert Informationen zum Reiseziel im Internet zu recherchieren. Direkt online buchbare Angebote und Bausteine qualifizieren die Präsentationen und erhöhen den Mehrwert einer jeden touristischen Internetseite. Dabei wird vorausgesetzt, dass die Qualität des Angebots über ein transparentes Preis-Leistungsverhältnis mit der Realität übereinstimmt und die Buchungsabwicklung sicher ist.

4.2 Die Nationalen Naturlandschaften[14]

Durch die Reiseanalyse der Forschungsgemeinschaft Urlaub und Reisen (F.U.R) wird bereits seit einigen Jahren bestätigt, dass eine intakte Natur und Umwelt bei mehr als 80 Prozent der Deutschen wichtig für die Reisezufriedenheit ist.[15]

Zu den beliebtesten Urlaubsformen gehören: 1. Urlaub in der Natur, 2. Städtereisen, 3. Aktivurlaub, 4. Gesundheitsurlaub. Neben den kulturtouristischen Themen der Städtereisen ist auch das Naturerlebnis für einen Aktivurlaub oder einen gesundheitsorientierten Urlaub in einer intakten Landschaft zentrales Element der touristischen Angebotsqualität. Dabei ist unter Natur(erlebnis)tourismus eine Form des Reisens in naturnahe Gebiete zu verstehen, bei dem das „Erleben" von Natur im Mittelpunkt steht.[16]

Bei dem Wort „Erleben" mag sich manchem natürlich sofort der Gedanke an die „Walking Safari" durch den Krüger Nationalpark in Südafrika oder an die Beobachtung von fischenden Grislybären in einem amerikanischen Großschutzgebiet aufdrängen. Doch auch in Deutschland gibt es eine Vielzahl von Landschaften, die mit ihrer naturräumlichen Einmaligkeit – zusammen mit Flora und Fauna – einem einzigartigen, besonderen Naturerlebnis gerecht werden.

---

[13] Deutsche Zentrale für Tourismus e.V., www.kurz-nah-weg.de, 16.02.2008

[14] Nationalen Naturlandschaften - die Idee, www.nationale-naturlandschaften.de/index.php?content=die-idee, 12.02.2008

[15] Reiseanalyse 2007, Forschungsgemeinschaft Urlaub und Reisen (F.U.R)

[16] Bundesamt für Naturschutz, www.bfn.de/0323_iyeoeko.html, 16.02.2008

Im Februar 2006 hat der Bundesminister für Umwelt, Naturschutz und Reaktorsicherheit, Sigmar Gabriel, eine EMNID-Studie vorgestellt, aus der hervorgeht, dass 88 Prozent der Befragten die Existenz von Großschutzgebieten[17], also von Nationalparks, Biosphärenreservaten und Naturparks, für wichtig bzw. sehr wichtig erachten. Jedoch kennen nur sechs Prozent der Befragten den Unterschied zwischen den verschiedenen Schutzgebietskategorien. Hier liegen das Problem und die Chance. Bis 2005 warben die deutschen Nationalparke, Biosphärenreservate und Naturparke getrennt um Besucher. Im Gegensatz zu den südafrikanischen „South African National Parks" oder dem „National Park Service" in den USA fehlte den deutschen Großschutzgebieten ein einheitliches Erscheinungsbild, ein Markenzeichen zur Visualisierung und eine Kommunikationsplattform.

Um die deutschen Großschutzgebiete besser präsentieren zu können, wurde von EUROPARC Deutschland in Kooperation mit dem Verband der Naturparke die Dachmarke „Nationale Naturlandschaften" geschaffen und im November 2005 vorgestellt. Sie wurde entwickelt, um die deutschen Großschutzgebiete zukünftig unter einem gemeinsamen Dach und in einem einheitlichen Erscheinungsbild zu präsentieren. Das macht es Interessierten leichter, sich zu informieren, da Auskünfte zu den deutschen Großschutzgebieten erstmals zentral zugänglich sind.

Abb. 2: Word-Bild-Marke[18]

---

[17] Bundesamt für Naturschutz: „Die in Deutschland geltenden Schutzgebietskategorien beruhen auf dem Bundesnaturschutzgesetz (BNatSchG). Die unterschiedlichen Schutzgebiete können hinsichtlich ihrer Größe, ihres Schutzzwecks und ihrer Schutzziele und den daraus abzuleitenden Nutzungseinschränkungen unterschieden werden ... Nationalparke, Biosphärenreservate und Naturparke werden aufgrund ihrer Flächengröße auch als Großschutzgebiete bezeichnet.", www.bfn.de/0308_gebietsschutz.html, 12.02.2008
[18] EUROPARC Deutschland Träger der Dachmarke Nationale Naturlandschaften

Auch der Deutsche Bundestag begrüßt diese Initiative „Nationale Naturlandschaften" und verlangt von der Bundesregierung die Förderung
konkreter Projekte und Publikationen. „Naturerlebnis" müsse zu einem
Markenzeichen des Deutschlandtourismus werden.[19] Nach einer weiteren EMNID-Umfrage vom Dezember 2006 im Auftrag von EURO-
PARC Deutschland würden sogar 62 Prozent der Deutschen einen In-
landsurlaub bevorzugt in den „Nationalen Naturlandschaften" verbringen.[20]

4.3 Das touristische Angebot der Nationalen Naturlandschaften

Die Nationalparke, Biosphärenreservate und Naturparke Deutschlands
halten Angebote vor, die den vorab genannten touristischen Trends in
Deutschland gerecht werden. Je nach Schutzstatus der Nationalen Naturlandschaft sind folgende Entwicklungen zu erkennen:

- Erlebnis- und Eventreisen:
  Steigerung der Erlebnis- und Genussorientierung z.b. Natur-Er-
  lebnis-Region Nationalpark Kellerwald-Edersee[21]
- Natur & Landschaft sowie Gesundheit & Wellness:
  Urlaub mit Erholung und Aktivität in einer intakten Natur, z.b. ak-
  tiv entspannen und kulinarisch genießen im Naturpark Altmühl-
  tal[22]
- Kulturtourismus:
  Sehenswürdigkeiten, historische Stätten, Deutschland im Wandel
  der Geschichte, z.b. in Städten wie Dessau und der Lutherstadt
  Wittenberg oder in den Gärten im Gartenreich Dessau-Wörlitz, im

---

[19] Deutscher Bundestag, Protokoll der 91. Sitzung des Deutschen Bundestages am
Donnerstag, dem 29. März 2007, Annahme der Beschlussempfehlung auf Druck-
sache 16/4269, www.bundestag.de/bic/a_prot/2007/ap16091.html, 12.02.2008

[20] EUROPARC Deutschland, Rückenwind für Nationale Naturlandschaften,
www.nationale-naturlandschaften.de/popup.php?content=news&newsid=3562&
was=news, 24.04.2007

[21] Nationalpark Kellerwald-Edersee, www.nationalpark-kellerwald-edersee.de,
12.02.2008

[22] Naturpark Altmühltal, www.naturpark-altmuehltal.de, 12.02.2008

sachsen-anhaltischen Teil des länderübergreifenden Biosphärenreservates Flusslandschaft Elbe[23]

- Messe-, Tagungs- und Kongresstourismus / Incentives: Deutschland als Ziel für Geschäftstourismus z.b. Der Tagungsharz = Tagen an besonderen Orten im National- und Naturpark Harz[24]

Diese Reisezielpräferenzen sind optimal für die Nationalen Naturlandschaften nutzbar und vor allem ausbaubar. Die Orientierung des naturtouristischen Marketings in den Großschutzgebieten an den beschriebenen Trends kann die positive Entwicklung der touristischen Ankünfte forcieren und die Zahl der Übernachtungen steigern. Somit werden auch die ökonomischen Effekte bei den Trägern von Großschutzgebieten und der dortigen Bevölkerung nachhaltig gesteigert. Mit dem prognostizierten wirtschaftlichen Mehrwert verbindet sich vor allem eine positive Verankerung der Nationalen Naturlandschaften einschließlich des Naturtourismus im Verständnis der Bevölkerung und der Politik.

Als wesentlichste Voraussetzung des Werbens um Kunden müssen sich die einzelnen Landesmarketingorganisationen (LMOs) und die Deutsche Zentrale für Tourismus (DZT) dem Thema der touristischen Inwertsetzung der Nationalen Naturlandschaften intensiver widmen. Es gilt, den Einfluss der Nationalen Naturlandschaften im Rahmen der Schwerpunktsetzung im touristischen Marketing der LMOs zu stärken. Ein entsprechendes Angebot von Seiten der Großschutzgebietsverwaltungen, aber auch der Naturschutzorganisationen, ist zu erarbeiten. Nur in enger Kooperation von Naturschutz und Tourismus können ökologische Konfliktpunkte entschärft und ökonomische Vorteile erwirkt werden. Bundesländer wie Brandenburg, Thüringen, Mecklenburg-Vorpommern und gerade auch Sachsen-Anhalt haben in der Bewerbung ihres naturräumlichen Potenzials in den letzten Jahren bereits Maßstäbe gesetzt.

Durch den Bundestagsbeschluss vom März 2007 fühlen sich die IMG, als Landesmarketingorganisation Sachsen-Anhalts und die TMG, als Vertriebspartner für touristische Dienstleistungen in ihren seit 2005 durchgeführten Maßnahmen, die sachsen-anhaltischen Nationalen Na-

---

[23] Biosphärenreservat Mittelbe, www.mittelelbe.com, www.gartenreich.net, 12.02.2008

[24] Der Tagungsharz, www.harztourismusmanagement.de/tagungsharz, 12.02.2008

turlandschaften nachhaltig touristisch in Wert zu setzen, bestärkt. Das „Naturreich Sachsen-Anhalt" wird aus diesem Grund auf hohem Niveau weiterentwickelt.

5. Das naturräumliche Potenzial des Landes[25]/[26]

5.1 Ausgangssituation

Abb. 3: Neun Nationale Naturlandschaften in Sachsen-Anhalt[27]

---

[25] Ministerium für Landwirtschaft und Umwelt Sachsen-Anhalt, http://www.sachsen-anhalt.de/LPSA/index.php?id=2201, 12.02.2008

[26] Tourismus-Marketing Sachsen-Anhalt GmbH, http://www.sachsen-anhalt-tourismus.de/xxl/de/764100/index.html, 12.02.2008

[27] Hoffmann und Partner Werbeagentur, Magdeburg

Sachsen-Anhalt hat mit seinen neun Großschutzgebieten (dem länderübergreifenden Nationalpark Harz, den beiden Biosphärenreservaten Mittelelbe und Südharz i. G. sowie den Naturparken Harz, Saale-Unstrut-Triasland, Unteres Saaletal, Dübener Heide, Fläming/Sachsen-Anhalt und Drömling) das Potenzial, um deutschlandweit einen qualitativ hochwertigen sowie naturnahen Tourismus in den Großschutzgebieten nach den Grundsätzen einer integrativen Tourismusförderung[28] zu etablieren. Ziel ist es, die in ihrer großen Vielfalt vorhandenen Naturräume unter marketingtechnischen Gesichtspunkten durch die Verknüpfung mit den touristischen Potenzialen des Landes Sachsen-Anhalt am Markt zu positionieren. Dafür spricht, dass immerhin mehr als 30 Prozent der Landesfläche von Großschutzgebieten geprägt werden. Der Bundesdurchschnitt liegt hier nur bei rund 20 Prozent. Mit den gegebenen räumlichen Bedingungen und hochwertigen Angeboten schafft Sachsen-Anhalt zu dem kulturellen ein weiteres Alleinstellungsmerkmal.

5.2 Die Alleinstellungsmerkmale der sachsenanhaltischen Großschutzgebiete

5.2.1 Der Nationalpark

Mitten in Deutschland, in der einzigartigen Mittelgebirgslandschaft des Harzes rings um den Brocken, liegt der bundesländerübergreifende Nationalpark Harz in Niedersachsen und Sachsen-Anhalt. Er ist der größte Waldnationalpark in Deutschland. Seine Aufgabe ist es, die Wunder der Natur für nachfolgende Generationen zu bewahren. Die Philosophie des Nationalparks Harz lässt sich an seinem Slogan erkennen: „Sagenumwobene Bergwildnis". Hier werden ökologische Kreisläufe zugelassen und für den Besucher des Parks auch verständlich und erlebbar gemacht. Die Mitarbeiter des Nationalparks leisten in den Nationalparkhäusern und auf den Erlebnispfaden „Löwenzahnpfad" und „Brockenstieg" eine hervorragende Arbeit.[29] Der Nationalpark ist Knotenpunkt für eine Vielzahl von Wander- und Radwanderwegen. So führt der „Harzer-Hexen-Stieg"[30] von Thale durch das Bodetal über den Brocken nach Osterode und um-

---

[28] Vgl. Kapitel 7 e.d.
[29] Nationalpark Harz, www.nationalpark-harz.de, 12.02.2008
[30] Harzer-Hexen-Stieg, www.harzer-hexen-stieg.de, 12.02.2008

gekehrt. Auch Mountainbiker kommen auf ihre Kosten. Rund 1.800 km Mountainbikerouten, teilweise auch durch den Nationalpark, führen durch den Harz, ohne dass sich Wanderer und Radfahrer gegenseitig behindern.[31] Gäste, die sich nicht aktiv im Nationalpark bewegen wollen oder können, haben dennoch die Chance, die Brockenkuppe zu erreichen. So führt die Brockenbahn der Harzer Schmalspurbahnen[32] direkt auf den Gipfel.

Wie eng Kultur und Natur hier im Nationalpark verwoben sind, lässt sich bei Goethe, der dem Harz und seinen Hexen im Faust ein Denkmal setzte, und bei Heinrich Heine in seiner Harzreise nachvollziehen.

Die „Nationalparkfreundlichen Unterkünfte" garantieren dem potenziellen Gast einen umweltgerechten und angenehmen Aufenthalt. Qualität, Erholung, Genuss und Gesundheit auf natürliche Weise werden in diesen Betrieben groß geschrieben.[33]

5.2.2 Biosphärenreservate

Biosphärenreservate stehen für gewachsene Kulturlandschaften, in denen Mensch und Natur im Einklang leben. In Sachsen-Anhalt befinden sich zwei Reservate.

- Seit 1979 existiert das UNESCO-Biosphärenreservat Mittelelbe mit dem größten zusammenhängenden Auenwald Europas. Es zieht sich entlang der Elbe durch Sachsen-Anhalt und ist Teil des bundesländerübergreifenden Biosphärenreservates Flusslandschaft Elbe.
  Das UNESCO-Welterbe Gartenreich Dessau-Wörlitz befindet sich im Biosphärenreservat Mittelelbe. Unter dem Motto „Weltkultur an wilden Ufern" wird deutlich, dass Fürst Leopold III. Friedrich Franz von Anhalt-Dessau es bereits im 18. Jahrhundert verstanden hat, Natur und Kultur in einen beispielhaften Kontext

---

[31] Harzer Verkehrsverband e.V., Harz Aktiv,
www.harzinfo.de/themen/index.php?th=1, 12.02.2008
[32] Harzer Schmalspurbahnen, www.hsb-wr.de, 12.02.2008
[33] In Deutschland werden z.Zt. in insgesamt fünf Nationalparken die nationalparkfreundlichen Unterkünfte unter dem Titel „Nationalpark Partner" präsentiert. Sie werden nach den Kriterien der Umweltdachmacke Viabono zertifiziert, www.nationalpark-partner.de, www.viabono.de, 12.02.2008

zu bringen. [34] Das Biosphärenreservat lässt sich am besten auf dem Elberadweg erkunden. [35] In der jährlichen Radanalyse des Allgemeinen Deutschen Fahrad-Club e.V. wird der Elberadweg schon seit mehreren Jahren als einer der beliebtesten Radfernwege Deutschlands geführt. Über diesen Weg lassen sich die einmaligen Kultur- und Naturlandschaften an der Elbe im wahrsten Sinne des Wortes erfahren. [36]

- Das Biosphärenreservat Karstlandschaft Südharz i. G. (in Gründung) [37] befindet sich im Südwesten Sachsen-Anhalts und stellt eine der bedeutendsten Gipskarstlandschaften in Europa dar. Zugleich ist die an Naturschönheiten reiche Landschaft auch eine einzigartige, durch eine neunhundertjährige Bergbautradition geprägte Kulturlandschaft, die sich über den „Karstwanderweg" erleben lässt. Dieser Weg führt durch den gesamten Südharz und verbindet Sachsen-Anhalt mit Thüringen und Niedersachsen. [38]

5.2.3 Die sechs Naturparke Sachsen-Anhalts

Naturparke sind großräumige Schutzgebiete, die sich mit ihren besonderen landschaftlichen Voraussetzungen für die Erholung in der und die Begegnung mit der Natur auszeichnen. Sie stellen eine seit Jahrhunderten durch schonende, angepasste landwirtschaftliche Nutzung geprägte Kulturlandschaft dar. „Schutz durch Nutzung" heißt das Konzept. Es gilt, dauerhaft umweltgerecht zu wirtschaften sowie Arten- und Biotopvielfalt zu erhalten. Deshalb fördern die Naturparke auch eine nachhaltige Form des Tourismus.

- Der Naturpark Harz umschließt das Gebiet des Nationalparks Harz. Mit dem Bodetal, der Teufelsmauer, den Rübeländer Tropf-

---

[34] Biosphärenreservat Mittelelbe, www.mittelelbe.com , www.gartenreich.net, 12.02.2008

[35] Der Elberadweg, www.elberadweg.de, 12.02.2008

[36] Allgemeiner Deutscher Fahrrad-Club e.V. - Radreiseanalyse 2007, www.adfc.de/4125_1, 12.02.2008

[37] Biosphärenreservat Karstlandschaft Südharz i. G., www.bioreskarstsuedharz.de, 12.02.2008

[38] Der Karstwanderweg, www.karstwanderweg.de, 12.02.2008

steinhöhlen oder den Schau- und Besucherbergwerken bietet sich nicht nur ein einmaliges Naturpanorama, sondern gleichzeitig ein Bilderbuch der deutschen Sagenwelt und Literaturgeschichte an. Der Naturpark gehört zum „Geopark Harz. Braunschweiger Land. Ostfalen" und ist als solcher in das Global Network of Geoparks aufgenommen. Geoparks helfen, das Erbe der Erdgeschichte zu bewahren und sind in sich selbst wieder touristische Höhepunkte. Im Naturpark hat eine Vielzahl von Wander- und Radwanderwegen ihren Startpunkt.[39]

- Im Naturpark Saale-Unstrut-Triasland wird seit dem 10. Jahrhundert Weinbau betrieben. Das Klima sowie die Gesteinsformationen, die sich im Trias vor 251 bis 206 Millionen Jahren gebildet haben, sind dem Weinanbau zuträglich. Der jahrhundertlange Abbau von Sandstein und Schaumkalk für Dome, Kirchen und Burgen hat geologisch interessante Aufschlüsse hinterlassen, die in vielen ausgeschilderten Geotopen und geologischen Lehrpfaden erlebbar sind. Im Naturpark befindet sich zudem auf dem Mittelberg im Ziegelrodaer Forst der Fundort der „Himmelsscheibe von Nebra". Die archäologische Weltsensation zeigt die älteste bekannte Himmelsdarstellung der Menschheit. Am Fundort wurde im Sommer 2007 als multimediales Erlebniscenter für die Bronzezeit die „Arche Nebra" eröffnet. Die Arche ist Bestandteil der neuen sachsen-anhaltischen touristischen Route „Himmelswege", die die archäologischen Sensationsfunde miteinander verbindet.[40] Aktiv lässt sich der Naturpark am besten auf den „Himmelswegen" und an bzw. auf den Gewässern des „Blauen Bandes" erkunden. Eine Kanutour auf Saale und Unstrut oder eine Radtour auf den flussbegleitenden Radwegen bietet dem Besucher eine wunderbare Perspektive auf die alte Kulturlandschaft.[41] Über den Saaleradwanderweg nach Halle ist der Anschluss an den Naturpark Unteres Saaletal gegeben. Somit lässt sich auch das Original der „Himmelsscheibe von Nebra" im Landesmuseum für Vorgeschichte in Halle (Saale) stressfrei erreichen.

---

[39] Naturpark Harz, www.harzregion.de, 12.02.2008
[40] Die Himmelswege, www.himmelswege.de, 12.02.2008
[41] Naturpark Saale-Unstrut-Triasland, www.naturpark-saale-unstrut.de, 12.02.2008

- Der Naturpark Unteres Saaletal umfasst im Zentrum Sachsen-Anhalts zwischen Halle und Bernburg eine aufregende und malerische Landschaft. Steil herausragende Felsen zeigen, mit welcher Kraft einst die Saale den Hettstedter Gebirgsrücken durchbrochen hat. Die ansteigenden Ackerflächen oder die vom Prallhang begrenzte Auenlandschaft mit Wiesen und Auwaldresten bietet Einblick in die erdgeschichtliche Evolution. Die südlichsten Großsteingräber Europas befinden sich hier.[42]

- Der länderübergreifende Naturpark Dübener Heide in Sachsen und Sachsen-Anhalt, einst Jagdgebiet der Adelshäuser zwischen Dresden und Oranienbaum, erstreckt sich zwischen den Flussauen von Elbe und Mulde. Kiefern- und Mischwälder prägen das größte zusammenhängende Waldgebiet des Mitteldeutschen Tieflands. Daneben steht die Vielfalt der Heidelandschaft, der Moore, Feuchtgebiete und Auenlandschaften. Diese abwechslungsreiche Landschaft gilt für die Ballungsräume um Halle und Leipzig als „Vorgarten". Vor allem die Moor- und Heilbäder im Naturpark – Bad Düben und Bad Schmiedeberg – gestatten mit ihren Angeboten die aktive und gesundheitsorientierte Erholung. Das Angebot der Direktvermarkter aus dem Naturpark „Bestes aus der Dübener Heide" ergänzt aktive Erholung mit gesunder Ernährung.

- Der Naturpark Fläming/Sachsen-Anhalt an der Grenze zu Brandenburg steht für eine alte Kulturlandschaft. Einst haben Holländer, Seeländer und Flamen mit ihren Erfahrungen bei der Entwässerung von Sumpfgebieten, der Anlage von Deichen sowie der Landbewirtschaftung das Gebiet urbar gemacht. In einer eiszeitlich geprägten Landschaft innerhalb der Norddeutschen Tiefebene spiegeln alte Burgen, Feldsteinkirchen und Mühlen die Geschichte wider. Durch die räumliche Nähe zu den UNESCO-Welterbestätten in Dessau und Wittenberg wird das Zusammenspiel von Kultur und Natur besonders deutlich. Der Naturpark bietet den Direktvermarktern und Gastronomen die Möglichkeit, mit dem Label „Naturpark Fläming/Sachsen-Anhalt" die kulinarischen High-

---

[42] Naturpark Unteres Saaletal, www.unteres-saaletal.de, 12.02.2008

lights, wie den „Fläming Korb" und den „Fläming Teller" zu bewerben.[43]

■ Der Naturpark Drömling im westlichen Teil der Altmark wird auch als „Land der tausend Gräben" bezeichnet. Es ist die von Menschen geschaffene alte preußische Kulturlandschaft, die dem Drömling seinen eigentümlichen Reiz gibt. Er bietet in der 800 ha großen Kernzone den letzten Lebensraum seltener Tiere, wie zum Beispiel Fischotter, Schrei- und Seeadler. Die Flora und Fauna des Naturparks lässt sich am besten bei naturkundlichen Touren zu Fuß oder auf dem Rad erleben.[44] Der Naturpark ist auch Bestandteil des „Grünen Bandes", der ehemaligen innerdeutschen Grenze und dem wahrscheinlich längsten Grünriegel der Welt. Das „Grüne Band" lässt sich als Denkmal für die Überwindung der deutschen Teilung ebenso erfahren, wie auch als ökologisches Highlight.[45]

6. Das „Naturreich Sachsen-Anhalt"

6.1 Der Nachfrage nach Natur gerecht werden

In Sachsen-Anhalt werden Themen- und Destinationsmarketing unter Berücksichtigung der bereits beschriebenen touristischen Trends konzentriert weiterentwickelt. Dabei sollen vor allem die Zahl der Übernachtungen und somit auch die ökonomischen Effekte nachhaltig gesteigert werden.

Die Stellung Sachsen-Anhalts als Kulturtourismus-Destination ist beschrieben. Nun gilt es, eine nachhaltige Vernetzung der touristischen Trends Kultur, Natur, Aktiv und Gesund voranzutreiben. Mit dem Projekt „Naturreich Sachsen-Anhalt" beantwortete die LMG Ende 2005 die Frage, in wie weit das naturräumliche Potenzial Sachsen-Anhalts touristisch in Wert gesetzt werden kann. Diese Idee wurde bereits seit Mitte 2004 verfolgt. Im Frühjahr 2005 begann die Realisierung des Projektes.

---

[43] Naturpark Fläming/Sachsen-Anhalt, www.naturpark-flaeming.de, 12.02.2008
[44] Naturpark Drömling, www.naturpark-droemling.de, 12.02.2008
[45] Das Grüne Band, www.dasgrueneband.info, 12.02.2008

In intensiver Zusammenarbeit zwischen der LMG und Vertretern der Ministerien für Landwirtschaft und Umwelt (MLU) sowie Wirtschaft und Arbeit (MWA), des Landesverwaltungsamtes (LVwA), der Großschutzgebiete, Touristikern, Naturschutzorganisationen sowie Marketingexperten wurden in konstruktiven Diskussionen die Inhalte des touristischen Projektes „Naturreich Sachsen-Anhalt" festgelegt. Dabei galt es, die unterschiedlichen Interessen abzuwägen und abzustimmen. Es war klar, dass dieser Diskussionsprozess nicht statisch zu betrachten ist, sondern unter Berücksichtigung des Marktes in den Folgejahren dynamisch weitergeführt werden muss.

Ausgangspunkt war die Reiseanalyse der Forschungsgemeinschaft Urlaub und Reisen (F.U.R) aus dem Jahr 2005, die ergab, dass für rund 84 Prozent der Deutschen intakte Natur und Umwelt wichtig für die Reisezufriedenheit sind. Dabei ist das Naturerlebnis in einer intakten Landschaft zentrales Element der touristischen Angebotsqualität. Natur soll mehr als nur eine Urlaubskulisse sein.[46] Passende Angebote, die diesem Anspruch gerecht werden, waren jedoch in Sachsen-Anhalt nicht bzw. nicht umfassend verfügbar. Hier lag der Ansatz für das Projekt „Naturreich Sachsen-Anhalt".

Zum Start der „Nationalen Naturlandschaften" und passend zum „Jahr der Naturparke 2006" wurden erstmalig Sachsen-Anhalts Großschutzgebiete mit thematisch abgestimmten touristischen Angeboten in einem gemeinsamen Druckwerk mit dem Titel „Naturreich Sachsen-Anhalt – Touristische Angebote zwischen Elbe, Harz, Saale und Unstrut" sowie im touristischen Internetportal des Landes Sachsen-Anhalt[47] dargestellt. Alle Großschutzgebiete des Landes, die Naturparke, der Nationalpark und die Biosphärenreservate werden als Ganzes präsentiert. Wichtig ist, um auch dem Bildungsaspekt gerecht zu werden, dass in der Broschüre in einer leicht verständlichen Art und Weise die Bedeutung sowie die Aufgaben jeder einzelnen Schutzgebietskategorie erläutert werden.

Ergänzend dazu wurden gleichrangig die Goitzsche bei Bitterfeld als Beispiel für einen beeindruckenden Renaturierungsprozess und das „Grüne Band", die ehemalige innerdeutsche Grenze, als verbindendes

---

[46] F.U.R Reiseanalyse 2005, www.fur.de/downloads/Reiseanalyse_2005.pdf, 12.02.2008

[47] Tourismus-Marketing Sachsen-Anhalt GmbH - Aktivitäten / Aktiv im Naturreich, www.sachsen-anhalt-tourismus.de/xxl/de/764100/index.html, 12.02.2008

Element zwischen fünf Großschutzgebieten, berücksichtigt. Aktivange-
bote in den Regionen des Landes sowie Informationen zur Erreichbar-
keit der touristischen Destinationen unter Benutzung des öffentlichen
Personennahverkehrs runden das Angebot ab. Zudem werden die wichtigsten Informationen zum „Naturreich" in Englischsprachigen Zusam-
menfassungen festgehalten.

Abb. 4: Naturreich Sachsen-Anhalt – Rollup für Präsentationen[48]

---

[48] Hoffmann und Partner Werbeagentur, Magdeburg

Das „Naturreich Sachsen-Anhalt" trägt dazu bei, das Bedürfnis nach Erholung in intakter Natur zu befriedigen. Durch touristische Angebote, in die Aspekte von Info- und Edutainment integriert sind, erfolgt zudem eine Sensibilisierung für den Natur- und Umweltschutz.

Pauschalangebote müssen in Zukunft noch stärker aus Sicht der Qualitätssicherung und -steigerung betrachtet werden, indem koordinierte und gezielte Schulungsmaßnahmen für Leistungsträger angeboten werden. Handbücher der Servicequalität Sachsen-Anhalt sowie der Ratgeber Produktentwicklung[49] sind dabei hilfreich. Auch der DTV bietet mit seinem „Naturerlebnisleitfaden" das entsprechende Handwerkszeug für die Erstellung von qualitativ hochwertigen Erlebnisangeboten, die Lust auf Natur machen.[50]

Im März 2007 erschien die zweite Auflage der Broschüre mit dem Titel „Naturreich Sachsen-Anhalt: Touristische Angebote in den Nationalen Naturlandschaften zwischen Elbe, Harz, Saale und Unstrut". Nachdem sich das „Naturreich Sachsen-Anhalt" zwei Jahre erfolgreich auf dem Markt bewährt hat, wurde im November 2007 die Weiterentwicklung und Qualifizierung beschlossen. Alle aktiv- und naturtouristischen Themen des Landes Sachsen-Anhalt sollen in Zukunft in einem Projekt zusammengeführt werden. So sollen Synergien sinnvoll genutzt werden, finden doch die wesentlichen aktivtouristischen Themen wie Wandern, Radwandern, Reiten oder Kanufahren in oder zwischen den Nationalen Naturlandschaften statt.

6.2 Die Weiterentwicklung: Aktiv im Naturreich Sachsen-Anhalt[51]

Das Zukunftsinstitut GmbH Kelkheim denkt im Jahr 2006 in seiner Studie „Tourismus 2020 – Die neuen Sehnsuchtsmärkte" über die künftigen Trends in der Tourismusbranche nach. Touristische Destinationen können sich in den kommenden Jahren nur am Markt profilieren, wenn

---

[49] Servicequalität Sachsen-Anhalt - Qualitätsoffensive für den Tourismus in Sachsen-Anhalt, www.servicequalitaet-sachsen-anhalt.de/admingate/site/download.php

[50] Deutscher Tourismusverband e.V., Leitfaden Naturerlebnisprodukte, www.deutschertourismusverband.de/index.php?pageId=62, 12.02.2008

[51] Ministerium für Wirtschaft und Arbeit, Handbuch Tourismus in Sachsen-Anhalt S. 59 ff, 2005

sie sich intensiver mit den Bedürfnissen des potenziellen Gastes auseinander setzen. Die Autoren der Studie beschreiben dabei die Reisesehnsucht als ein Grundmotiv der menschlichen Existenz, welches sich gegenwärtig neu konstituiert.[52]

„… nur wer imstande ist, die Veränderungen in der Bedürfnisökonomie seiner Kunden frühzeitig zu deuten, wird auf den Märkten von morgen zu den Gewinnern gehören", schließen die Kelkheimer. „Und die Urlauber der Zukunft erfordern unsere ganze Aufmerksamkeit und Kreativität. Sie lassen sich nicht mehr wie bisher über den üblichen Leisten der Marktforschung nach Demografie, Geschlecht oder Einkommen schlagen. Der touristische Mentalitätswechsel, den wir gegenwärtig erleben, konfrontiert uns mit teils paradoxen Wünschen und Verhaltensweisen" verkünden Eike Wenzl und Anja Kirig. Weg von der bloßen Bedürfnisbefriedigung, hin zum Stillen von Sehnsüchten, beschreiben die Autoren den von ihnen erwarteten Paradigmenwechsel.

Auch unsere Marktbeobachtungen (siehe auch die Ergebnisse der Permanenten Gästebefragungen Sachsen-Anhalt in den Jahren 2001/2002 und 2006/07[53]) bestätigen – zumindest partiell – diese Erkenntnisse und halten zu Schlussfolgerungen gerade für die Angebote der aktiv- und naturtouristischen Potenziale Sachsen-Anhalts an.

Zu den am weitesten verbreiteten Aktivitäten in der Natur zählen Wandern, Radwandern und der Wassersport, der mit dem „Blauen Band" ja bereits eine Markensäule im Tourismus Sachsen-Anhalts darstellt. Das „Blaue Band" subsumiert dabei als aktivtouristische Markensäule alle Angebote auf oder an den sachsen-anhaltischen Gewässern und stellt so die Verbindung zu den anderen Markensäulen und Schwerpunktthemen im aktivtouristischen Verständnis dar.

Bei entsprechenden klimatischen Bedingungen ist der Wintersport im Harz weit verbreitet.

Für den Reittourismus sind in ganz Sachsen-Anhalt, insbesondere in der Altmark aber auch in Anhalt-Wittenberg, exzellente Bedingungen und eine entsprechende Infrastruktur vorhanden, die weiter ausgebaut wird.

---

[52] Zukunftsinstitut, Tourismus 2020, www.zukunftsinstitut.de/downloads/rez_tourismus2020_MountainManager_022 006.pdf, 17.02.2008

[53] IMG, Permanente Gästebefragung 2006/07 Sachsen-Anhalt, http://www.img-sachsen-anhalt.de/?cid=119009003383, 17.02.2008

Die Angebote lassen sich vielfältig mit anderen Aktivitäten verknüpfen. Objekte an der „Straße der Romanik" dienen als Ziel einer Wandertour. Aber auch die Markensäule „Gartenträume" bietet weitere Möglichkeiten.

Die neue Pilgerleidenschaft der Deutschen als Ausdruck des Strebens nach Selbstfindung und Einssein mit der Umwelt im weitesten Sinne ist mehr als der Ausdruck eines spirituell motivierten Tourismus, wiewohl auch diese Motivation erkennbar zunimmt. Sachsen-Anhalt bietet dafür mit einer spannenden Etappe des Jakobsweges aber auch mit dem neuen „Lutherweg" ausbaufähiges Potenzial.

Die überregionalen Radwege Sachsen-Anhalts, allen voran der Elberadweg als beliebtester Radweg Deutschlands[54], bieten ebenfalls zahlreiche Möglichkeiten der touristischen Vernetzung. Gerade diese Kombination von Radelaktivitäten mit kulturellen Sehenswürdigkeiten ist ein großer Marktvorteil, da bei den Radwanderern nicht die sportlichen Ambitionen im Vordergrund stehen, sondern das Besichtigen in Verbindung mit guten Einkehrmöglichkeiten. Abseits des Harzes ermöglichen die naturräumlichen Gegebenheiten in Sachsen-Anhalt zudem ein bequemes Radeln ohne größere Steigungen.

Die wesentlichen sachsen-anhaltischen Wasserwege, Wander- und Radwanderwege sowie Reitrouten liegen entweder in einem Großschutzgebiet, sind verbindendes Element zwischen den Naturlandschaften oder werden durch besondere Landschaften abseits der Schutzgebiete geprägt.

Um dem interessierten Gast Informationen zu den benannten Natur- und Aktivthemen und deren direkter Vernetzung zum kulturtouristischen Angebot zur Verfügung zu stellen, ist die Qualifizierung der vorhandenen Informations- und Angebotsbroschüren von IMG und TMG in vollem Gange. Eine Weiterentwicklung der zum Thema passenden Internetseiten unter „www.sachsen-anhalt-tourismus.de" geht damit einher.

„Aktiv im Naturreich Sachsen-Anhalt" wird die Inhalte der vorhandenen Broschüren „Blaues Band – Wassertourismus in Sachsen-Anhalt", „Radwandern in Sachsen-Anhalt" und „Naturreich Sachsen-Anhalt" zu einem attraktiven Ganzen verknüpfen. Die Nationalen Naturlandschaften Sachsen-Anhalts werden so in den direkten Bezug zum kultur- und aktivtouristischen Angebot gebracht.

---

[54] vgl. S. 12 e.d.

Abb. 5: „Aktiv im Naturreich Sachsen-Anhalt" mit Beileger

Die neue Broschüre „Aktiv im Naturreich Sachsen-Anhalt" (Hg. TMG) wird als Image- und Informationsbroschüre aufgestellt. In einem Beileger (Hg. TMG) zur Broschüre werden die attraktiven buchbaren touristischen Angebote der Leistungsträger in entsprechender Qualität dargestellt.[55]

Um eine möglichst weite Verbreitung der Angebote über alle Vermarktungsschienen zu erreichen, ist die Onlinebuchbarkeit der Angebote wünschenswert. Wenn diese Buchbarkeit gegeben ist, können die sachsen-anhaltischen Naturlandschaften die touristischen Angebote aus ihrem Gebiet über ihre eigenen Internetpräsentationen kommunizieren und durch Einbindung der in Sachsen-Anhalt benutzten Onlinebuchungsplattform über eine Vermittlungsprovision Einnahmen generieren.

Parallel zur Broschüre „Aktiv im Naturreich Sachsen-Anhalt" wird es eine Rad- und Freizeitkarte Sachsen-Anhalt (Hg. IMG) geben. Darüber hinaus wird für den Wassertouristen eine separate Karte erstellt, in der die vorhandene Infrastruktur am Blauen Band wie beispielsweise

---

[55] vgl. Kap. 6.1 ed.

Anlegestellen, Rastplätze, Häfen, Entsorgungsstellen und Sehenswürdigkeiten dargestellt wird.

Mit der beschriebenen Qualifizierung des Informationsmaterials und der damit einhergehenden Aufwertung des touristischen Angebots braucht Sachsen-Anhalt auch in den nächsten Jahren den Wettbewerb im Deutschlandtourismus nicht zu scheuen.

7. Empfehlung und Abschlussbetrachtung

7.1 Großschutzgebiete und das System des Integrativen Tourismus

Im Jahr 1992 wurde die Agenda 21 auf der Konferenz für Umwelt und Entwicklung der Vereinten Nationen in Rio de Janeiro verabschiedet.[56] Zehn Jahre nach Rio wurde auf dem Weltgipfel für Nachhaltige Entwicklung in Johannesburg 2002 Bilanz gezogen und geprüft, in wie weit die Ziele der Agenda erreicht wurden. Zudem wurde über das Leitbild der nachhaltigen Entwicklung in Zeiten der Globalisierung beraten.[57]

Auf Empfehlung des Weltgipfels in Johannesburg rief die Vollversammlung der Vereinten Nationen im Dezember 2002 für die Jahre 2005 bis 2014 eine Weltdekade „Bildung für nachhaltige Entwicklung" aus. Ihr Ziel ist es, durch Bildungsmaßnahmen zur Umsetzung der in Rio beschlossenen und in Johannesburg bekräftigten Agenda 21 beizutragen und die Prinzipien nachhaltiger Entwicklung weltweit in den nationalen Bildungssystemen zu verankern. Dabei geht es um die Förderung der Schulbildung, des öffentlichen Bewusstseins und der beruflichen Aus- und Fortbildung.[58] Die Dekade stellt damit die erste offizielle Verknüpfung von nachhaltiger Entwicklung mit der Bildung dar.[59]

---

[56] Agenda 21 - www.bmz.de/de/themen/umwelt/hintergrund/umweltpolitik/rio_1992.html, 12.02.2008
[57] Johannesburg 2002, www.bmz.de/de/themen/umwelt/hintergrund/umweltpolitik/johannesburg.html, 12.02.2008
[58] Bundesministerium für Umwelt, Naturschutz und Reaktorsicherheit (Hrg.), Agenda 21, S. 280 (1992)
[59] UN-Weltdekade „Bildung für nachhaltige Entwicklung (2005-2014)", www.bne-portal.de, 12.02.2008

Im Ergebnis von Rio und Johannesburg sowie den vereinbarten Zielen der UN-Weltdekade sollte sich der Tourismus in Großschutzgebieten am System des Integrativen Tourismus orientieren. Einen praxisnahen Vorschlag bietet das in Wien ansässige „Institut für Integrativen Tourismus und Entwicklung – respect".

In einer umfassenden Definition werden die Dimensionen der Nachhaltigkeit integrativ, also als ein systematisches Ganzes betrachtet. Das Institut legt bei der Diskussion um eine nachhaltige Entwicklung im und durch den Tourismus sechs Prämissen fest, die bei der Umsetzung von Tourismusvorhaben in Großschutzgebieten, aber auch für Entwicklung eines naturnahen Tourismus außerhalb dieser Gebiete, Beachtung finden müssen: [60]

1. ökologische Dimension – intakter Lebens-, Kultur- und Naturraum ist die Voraussetzung für den Tourismus der Zukunft
2. ökonomische Dimension – Tourismus muss eingebettet sein in eine sektorübergreifende, regionsspezifisch vernetzte Wirtschaft
3. sozio-kulturelle Dimension – Urlaubsregionen werden geprägt von selbstbestimmter kultureller Dynamik und sozialer Zufriedenheit der Bevölkerung sowie der im Tourismus Arbeitenden
4. institutionelle Dimension – das Individuum als Gestalter von Tourismuspolitik
5. Entwicklung betrieblicher und kommunaler Umweltmanagementsysteme sowie Nachhaltigkeitsstrategien für intensiv genutzte touristische Destinationen, wobei sich die Tourismuspolitik den ökologischen und sozialen Problemen des Massentourismus stellen muss
6. steigende Verantwortung der Quellgebiete und übergeordneter politischer Systeme – das heißt, Probleme, die durch den Tourismus entstehen, sind nicht nur durch die Urlaubsdestinationen zu verantworten, sondern auch durch die Touristen selbst

Die neuen Formen des Reisens müssen sich auch mit der Lösung vorhandener Probleme beschäftigen. Hierbei soll der Blick fürs Ganze geschärft werden. Es ist wichtig, die einzelnen Schritte der Entwicklung

---

[60] respect (2003) - Institut für Integrativen Tourismus und Entwicklung, www.respect.at/content.php?id=193&m_id=1, 12.02.2008

nicht nur von außen zu koordinieren, sondern in vorhandene Strukturen einzelner Regionen zu integrieren. Workshops vor Ort können dabei sehr hilfreich sein.

Die Anforderungen des „integrativen Tourismus" verlangen koordinierte Handlungsabläufe durch Netzwerkbildungen der Akteure. Besonders hervorzuheben ist hier die Beteiligung des Nationalparks Harz an der „Internationalen Charta für einen nachhaltigen Tourismus in Schutzgebieten".[61]

7.2 Naturreich Sachsen-Anhalt: Ein Ausblick

Das Echo auf das Projekt „Naturreich Sachsen-Anhalt", sowohl von Naturschutzexperten, Touristikern, aber vor allen von Endkunden zeigt, dass die konsequente Umsetzung des Projektes unter Leitung der Landesmarketingorganisation in den Jahren 2005 und 06 eine richtige Entscheidung war. Die Erfahrungen aus dem Projekt sind für die Entwicklung der „Nationalen Naturlandschaften" auf Bundesebene als „Best-Practice-Beispiel" unverzichtbar.

Als Zeichen der Nachhaltigkeit der Maßnahmen installierte die LMG im Dezember 2005 den Marketingbeirat Natur, der die LMG bei ihren Marketingaktivitäten unterstützt. Im Beirat waren Vertreter von Ministerien, des Landesverwaltungsamtes, der Großschutzgebiete, Touristiker, Naturschutzorganisationen sowie Marketingexperten tätig.

Mit der Neuausrichtung des sachsen-anhaltischen Tourismus und der Konzentration der Angebote auf die Bereiche „Natur und Aktiv" wurde der Marketingbeirat im Februar 08 umstrukturiert. Der neue Beirat „Natur- und Aktivtourismus" legt unter Federführung der IMG in einer intensiven Zusammenarbeit und konstruktiven Diskussion die Inhalte der Marketingaktivitäten im Bereich „Natur- und Aktivtourismus in Sachsen-Anhalt" fest. Konstituierende Mitglieder sind: die TMG, Vertreter der Ministerien für Landwirtschaft und Umwelt (MLU), für Wirtschaft und Arbeit (MWA) sowie für Landesentwicklung und Verkehr (MLV), des Landesverwaltungsamtes (LVwA), der neun Großschutzgebiete, der Koordinierungsstellen der wichtigsten Radfernwege Sachsen-Anhalts, der Verein Blaues Band, der ADFC, die Nahverkehrsgesellschaft Sachsen-

---

[61] www.european-charter.org, 12.02.2008

Anhalt mbH/Deutsche Bahn, die Naturschutzorganisationen, der Deutschen Wanderverband/Sachsen-Anhalt sowie Marketingexperten.

Um den ständig steigenden Qualitätsansprüchen des Marktes gerecht zu werden, müssen die touristischen Leistungsträger die Qualität ihrer „Erlebnisangebote" regelmäßig überprüfen und neue Angebote entwickeln.

Im Ergebnis steht die Erkenntnis, dass es eine zentrale Schnittstelle geben muss, die die Sprache der Touristiker spricht und die der Naturschützer versteht und natürlich umgekehrt. Nur so kann es gelingen, das neue Projekt „Aktiv im Naturreich Sachsen-Anhalt" zu etablieren.

Das Reiseland Sachsen-Anhalt steckt voller Überraschungen, informieren Sie sich unter: www.sachsen-anhalt-tourismus.de

Dipl. Kaufm. (FH)
Matthias Poeschel
Projektmanager
Tourismus-Marketing Sachsen-Anhalt GmbH
Am Alten Theater 6
D-39104 Magdeburg

Tel.: ++49-391-567-7074
Fax: ++49-391-567-7081
Email: matthias.poeschel@tmg-sachsen-anhalt.de

Quellen- und Literaturverzeichnis

Bundesministerium für Umwelt, Naturschutz und Reaktorsicherheit (Hg.) (1992): *Agenda 21*. Bonn.

Forschungsgemeinschaft Urlaub und Reisen (F.U.R) (2007): *Reiseanalyse 2007*. Kiel.

Forschungsgemeinschaft Urlaub und Reisen (F.U.R) (2005): *Reiseanalyse 2005*. Kiel.

Landesmarketing Sachsen-Anhalt GmbH (2004): *Landesmarketing Sachsen-Anhalt GmbH 1999-2003*. Magdeburg.

Landesmarketing Sachsen-Anhalt GmbH (Hg.) (2004): *MASTERPLAN TOURIS-MUS – Handlungsstrategie 2004-2008*. Magdeburg.

Ministerium für Wirtschaft und Arbeit des Landes Sachsen-Anhalt (Hg.) (2005): *Handbuch Tourismus in Sachsen-Anhalt*. Magdeburg.

Internetquellenverzeichnis

Allgemeiner Deutscher Fahrrad-Club e.V. (2007): *Radreiseanalyse 2007*. 12.02.2008. www.adfc.de/4125_1

Biosphärenreservat Karstlandschaft Südharz i. G..12.02.2008. www.bioreskarstsuedharz.de

Biosphärenreservat Mittelelbe. 12.02.2008. www.mittelelbe.com, www.gartenreich.net

Bundesamt für Naturschutz (2008): *Definition Großschutzgebiete*. 12.02.2008. www.bfn.de/0308_gebietsschutz.html

Bundesamt für Naturschutz: *Definition Naturtourismus*. 16.02.2008. www.bfn.de/0323_iyeoeko.html

Bundesministerium für wirtschaftliche Zusammenarbeit und Entwicklung: *Agenda 21 – ES BEGANN IN RIO 1992*. 12.02.2008. www.bmz.de/de/themen/umwelt/hintergrund/umweltpolitik/rio_1992.html

Bundesministerium für wirtschaftliche Zusammenarbeit und Entwicklung: *Johannesburg 2002*. 12.02.2008. www.bmz.de/de/themen/umwelt/hintergrund/umweltpolitik/johannesburg. html

Deutsche Zentrale für Tourismus e.V. (2008): *Kurz-Nah-Weg*. 16.02.2008. www.kurz-nah-weg.de

Matthias Poeschel

Deutsche UNESCO-Kommission: *UN-Weltdekade "Bildung für nachhaltige Entwicklung (2005-2014)"*. 12.02.2008.
www.bne-portal.de

Deutscher Bundestag (29.03.2007): *Protokoll der 91. Sitzung des Deutschen Bundestages.* 12.02.2008.
www.bundestag.de/bic/a_prot/2007/ap16091.html

Deutscher Tourismusverband e.V. (2006): *Leitfaden Naturerlebnisprodukte.* 12.02.2008.
www.deutschertourismusverband.de/index.php?pageId=62

Elberadweg. 12.02.2008.
www.elberadweg.de

EUROPARC Deutschland (2007): *Rückenwind für Nationale Naturlandschaften.* 12.02.2008.
www.nationale-naturlandschaften.de/popup.php?content=news&newsid=3562&was=news

EUROPARC Federation*: European Charter for Sustainable Tourism in Protected Areas.* 12.02.2008.
www.european-charter.org

Grünes Band. 12.02.2008.
www.dasgrueneband.info

Investitions- und Marketinggesellschaft Sachsen-Anhalt mbH (2008): *Die IMG – Ihr Partner* in *Sachsen-Anhalt.* 12.02.2008.
www.img-sachsen-anhalt.de/index.php?id=119009000003

Investitions- und Marketinggesellschaft Sachsen-Anhalt mbH (26.11.2007): *Permanente Gästebefragung 2006/07 Sachsen-Anhalt.* 17.02.2008.
www.img-sachsen-anhalt.de/?cid=119009003383

Harzer Verkehrsverband e.V.: *Harz Aktiv.* 12.02.2008.
www.harzinfo.de/themen/index.php?th=1

Harzer Verkehrsverband e.V.: *Der Tagungsharz.* 12.02.2008.
www.harztourismusmanagement.de/tagungsharz

Harzer Schmalspurbahnen. 12.02.2008.
www.hsb-wr.de

Harzer-Hexen-Stieg. 12.02.2008.
www.harzer-hexen-stieg.de

Die Himmelswege. 12.02.2008.
www.himmelswege.de

Karstwanderweg. 12.02.2008.
www.karstwanderweg.de

Land Sachsen-Anhalt (2008): *Standortkampagne*. 17.02.2008.
www.sachsen-anhalt.de/LPSA/index.php?id=Standortkampagne

Landesverwaltungsamt (LvwA) Sachsen-Anhalt: *Großschutzgebiete*. 12.02.2008.
www.sachsen-anhalt.de/LPSA/index.php?id=11205

Ministerium für Landwirtschaft und Umwelt Sachsen-Anhalt: *Nationalpark Harz*.
12.02.2008.
www.sachsen-anhalt.de/LPSA/index.php?id=2201

Nationalen Naturlandschaften (2008): *Die Idee*. 12.02.2008.
www.nationale-naturlandschaften.de/index.php?content=die-idee

Nationalpark Harz. 12.02.2008.
www.nationalpark-harz.de

Nationalpark Kellerwald-Edersee. 12.02.2008.
www.nationalpark-kellerwald-edersee.de

Naturpark Altmühltal. 12.02.2008.
www.naturpark-altmuehltal.de

Naturpark Drömling, 12.02.2008.
www.naturpark-droemling.de

Naturpark Fläming / Sachsen-Anhalt. 12.02.2008.
www.naturpark-flaeming.de

Naturpark Harz. 12.02.2008.
www.harzregion.de

Naturpark Saale-Unstrut-Triasland. 12.02.2008.
www.naturpark-saale-unstrut.de

Naturpark Unteres Saaletal, 12.02.2008.
www.unteres-saaletal.de

respect - Institut für Integrativen Tourismus und Entwicklung (2003): *Intergrativer Tourismus*. 12.02.2008.
www.respect.at/content.php?id=193&m_id=1

Servicequalität Sachsen-Anhalt: *Qualitätsoffensive für den Tourismus in Sachsen-Anhalt*.
12.02.2008.
www.servicequalitaet-sachsen-anhalt.de/admingate/site/download.php

Statistisches Landesamt Sachsen-Anhalt Halle (Saale) (2008): *Beherbergungen im Reiseverkehr – Jahresdaten 2001 – 2006*. 17.02.2008.
www.statistik.sachsen-anhalt.de/Internet/Home/Daten_und_Fakten/4/45/455/45511/Beherbergungen_Jahesangaben.html

Statistisches Landesamt Sachsen-Anhalt Halle (Saale) (2008): *Ankünfte und Übernachtungen im Reiseverkehr Monatsdaten für das Berichtsjahr 2007*, 11.06.2008.
www.stala.sachsen-anhalt.de/Internet/Home/Veroeffentlichungen/Pressemitteilungen/2008/03/36.html.

Tourismus-Marketing Sachsen-Anhalt GmbH: *Das Naturreich Sachsen-Anhalt*. 12.02.2008.
www.sachsen-anhalt-tourismus.de/xxl/de/764100/index.html

Tourismus-Marketing Sachsen-Anhalt GmbH (2008): *TMG intern*. 17.02.2008.
www.sachsen-anhalt-tourismus.de

Zukunftsinstitut (2006): *Tourismus 2020*. 17.02.2008.
www.zukunftsinstitut.de/downloads/rez_tourismus2020_MountainManager_02 2006.pdf

Nationalpark Wattenmeer und Tourismus
- Erfolgreiche Kooperation für Mensch und Natur

Christiane Gätje & Maren Babinsky

1. Einführung

Naturschutz und Tourismus werden immer noch eher als Gegensätze denn als potentielle Partner wahrgenommen. Die Vereinbarkeit beider Bereiche – der eine auf den Schutz der Landschaft, der Pflanzen, der Tiere und der ökologischen Prozesse fokussiert, der andere auf wirtschaftliche Interessen ausgerichtet – wird in Konzepten des nachhaltigen Tourismus verfolgt. Angestrebt wird, touristische Aktivitäten und Entwicklungen so auszugestalten, dass die Natur als eine der wichtigsten Grundlagen des Tourismus geschützt und erhalten bleibt und dennoch für die Menschen erlebbar ist. Eine Einbindung und Beteiligung regionaler Akteure und touristischer Leistungsträger ist dabei selbstverständlich. Vielfältige und attraktive Naturerlebnis-Angebote für Urlauber – draußen und drinnen, nach dem Motto „Betreten, bestaunen und anfassen erlaubt!", Natur genießen, Wildnis erleben, Spezial-Offerten für Naturinteressierte, eine breite Palette von Bildungsangeboten für Kinder und Erwachsene – damit eröffnet sich auch eine wirtschaftliche Perspektive. Naturschutz und Tourismus können gemeinsam zum Impulsgeber nachhaltiger Regionalentwicklung werden.

Wie eine solch produktive Partnerschaft aussehen kann, welch beiderseitiger Nutzen sich daraus ergibt, und welche Herausforderungen damit verbunden sind, soll am Beispiel des Nationalparks Schleswig-Holsteinisches Wattenmeer aufgezeigt werden.

2. „EUROPARC - Nationale Naturlandschaften"

Naturschutz ist in Deutschland Ländersache. Vor diesem Hintergrund gründete sich 1991 EUROPARC Deutschland, damals als FÖNAD, als gemeinnützige Organisation, die eine länderübergreifende Koordinierung von Großschutzgebieten in der Bundesrepublik anstrebt. Als Dachverband für Nationalparks, Biosphärenreservate und Naturparks vertritt

EUROPARC Deutschland das Ziel, diese zu schützen und zu erhalten. Nach dem EUROPARC-Leitbild sind Großschutzgebiete...

„...geschützte Landschaften, die das Naturerbe für Mensch und Natur bewahren und entwickeln. Sie sichern die Lebensräume von Mensch und Natur durch den Schutz von Boden, Wasser und Luft sowie von Lebensgemeinschaften der Tiere und Pflanzen und sie wirken mit bei der behutsamen Entwicklung der gewachsenen Natur- und Kulturlandschaften." (EUROPARC 2005, 9)

Unter der Dachmarke Nationale Naturlandschaften werden die bundesweit 14 Nationalparks, 13 Biosphärenreservate und eine Reihe von Naturparks gemeinsam präsentiert, um auf die Naturschönheiten Deutschlands und ihre touristische Attraktivität aufmerksam zu machen. Dieses Anliegen unterstützt das Bundesumweltministerium, wie den Worten der Parlamentarischen Staatssekretärin, Astrid Klug, zu entnehmen ist:

„Die Entwicklung der Marke Nationale Naturlandschaften ist ein Baustein in den Bemühungen, den Tourismusstandort Deutschland aufzubessern. Die Stärkung des Inlandtourismus ist aus ökonomischer und ökologischer Sicht sinnvoll. Denn wenn Natur zum Ziel für Touristen wird, dann erhält sie auch einen wirtschaftlichen Wert." (BMU & EUROPARC 2007)

2.1 Nationalparks in Deutschland

Im Bundesnaturschutzgesetz stellen Nationalparks die höchste Schutzkategorie dar und sind definiert als

„rechtsverbindlich festgesetzte einheitlich zu schützende Gebiete, die
1. großräumig und von besonderer Eigenart sind,
2. in einem überwiegenden Teil ihres Gebiets die Voraussetzungen eines Naturschutzgebiets erfüllen und,
3. sich in einem überwiegenden Teil ihres Gebiets in einem vom Menschen nicht oder wenig beeinflussten Zustand befinden oder geeignet sind, sich in einen Zustand zu entwickeln oder in einen Zustand entwickelt zu werden, der einen möglichst ungestörten Ablauf der Naturvorgänge in ihrer natürlichen Dynamik gewährleistet." (BNatSchG § 24, Abs. 1, 2006)

Der erste Nationalpark in Deutschland war der 1970 eingerichtete Nationalpark Bayerischer Wald. Die 14 Nationalparks in Deutschland folgen dem EUROPARC Deutschland-Leitbild: Nationalparks sind Landschaften, in denen Natur Natur bleiben darf, oder kurz: „Natur Natur sein lassen".

Nationalparks symbolisieren jedoch keineswegs nur unberührte Natur, sie dienen als Erfahrungsräume für Naturerleben und sind unerlässlich für Umweltbildung und Forschung. Zudem prägen Nationalparks stark das Erscheinungsbild einer Region und sind zu einem wichtigen Faktor der regionalen Wirtschaft geworden. Sie fördern den naturverbundenen Tourismus und steigern die Nachfrage nach regionalen Angeboten. Im Nationalpark soll der Naturschutz mit den Menschen im gemeinsamen Interesse von Mensch und Natur stattfinden (EUROPARC 2005).

2.2 Nationalpark Schleswig-Holsteinisches Wattenmeer

Das Wattenmeer erstreckt sich entlang der Nordseeküste Dänemarks und Deutschlands bis zu den Niederlanden über ein Areal von 9.300 km² und ist mit seinen weiten Schlick- und Sandwattflächen, Sandbänken und Stränden die größte kohärente Wattenlandschaft der Welt mit natürlichen dynamischen Prozessen, die in einer weitgehend ungestörten Natur ablaufen. So gilt es zu Recht als eines der letzten Gebiete europäischer Wildnis, dass weitgehend dem menschlichen Einfluss entzogen ist. Um dieses einzigartige marine, tidegeprägte Ökosystem in seiner besonderen Eigenart, Schönheit und Ursprünglichkeit zu bewahren, wurde es in Deutschland an der schleswig-holsteinischen Küste 1985 zum National-park erklärt. 1986 folgte die Ausweisung in Niedersachsen und 1990 auch in Hamburg, somit steht fast die gesamte deutsche Wattenmeerre-gion unter Schutz.

Der Nationalpark Schleswig-Holsteinisches Wattenmeer ist mit einer Ausdehnung von der dänischen Grenze bis zur Elbmündung mit 135 Kilometern Länge, von den Deichen zur offenen Nordsee mit 55 Kilometern Breite und einer Fläche von 4.415 km² nicht nur der größte der drei Wattenmeer-Nationalparks, sondern auch der größte in Mitteleuro-pa. Festland und Inseln haben eine Gesamtküstenlänge von 460 Kilome-tern (Abb. 1).

Das schleswig-holsteinische Wattenmeer erfüllt mehrere internationale Kriterien für Schutzgebiete. So ist es nicht nur als Nationalpark ausge-wiesen, sondern auch als NATURA 2000-Gebiet nach der EU-Vogel-schutz-Richtlinie und Flora-Fauna-Habitat-Richtlinie und gilt als eines der wichtigsten internationalen Feuchtbiotope nach der Ramsar-Kon-vention.

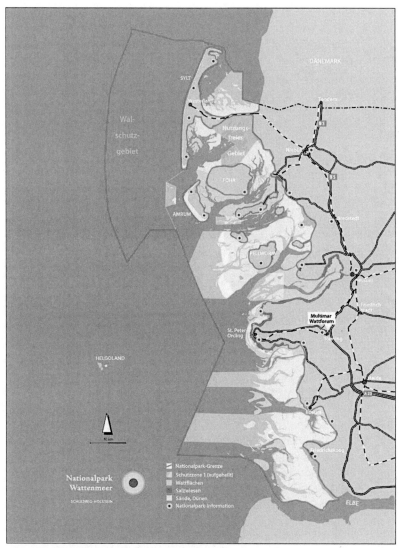

Abb. 1: Nationalparkgrenzen und Schutzzonen[1]

---

[1] Quelle: Nationalparkverwaltung Schleswig-Holsteinisches Wattenmeer

1990 erfolgte die Anerkennung des Schleswig-Holsteinischen Wattenmeeres als Biosphärenreservat durch die UNESCO, seit 2005 trägt es
nach einer Erweiterung durch den Beitritt der Halligen den Namen
„Biosphärenreservat Schleswig-Holsteinisches Wattenmeer und Halligen".
Geprägt durch einmalige Salzwiesen (Abb. 2), ausgedehnte Wattflächen, Priele, Sandbänke, Strände und Dünen ist das Wattenmeer ein be-
deutender Naturraum mit einer außergewöhnlich hohen biologischen
Produktion und Artenvielfalt. Die bei Ebbe so leblos erscheinenden
Wattflächen bergen angepasste Spezialisten der Bodenfauna, deren Bio-
masse die des Tropenwaldes übertrifft. Rund 3.200 Tierarten leben im
Wattenmeer, darunter zahlreiche Arten die nur in den Salzwiesen des
Wattenmeeres existieren. Das bedeutendste Säugetier im schleswig-holsteinischen Wattenmeer ist der Seehund, rund 8.000 Vertreter dieser
Robbenart leben hier. Auch Kegelrobben und Schweinswale (die einzige
einheimische Walart) finden ihren Lebensraum im Wattenmeer. Für letz-
tere wurde ein Walschutzgebiet vor der Westküste von Sylt und Amrum
eingerichtet, nachdem dort besonders viele Weibchen mit Jungen gesich-
tet wurden.

Abb. 2: Salzwiese mit blühenden Strandastern im Nationalpark[2]

[2] Quelle: Nationalparkverwaltung Schleswig-Holsteinisches Wattenmeer, Stock

Das Wattenmeer ist, bedingt durch die hohe Biomasseproduktion, wesentliches Brut-, Nahrungs-, Rast- und Durchzugsgebiet für etwa 25 Zugvogelarten der Ostatlantikroute und damit eines der vogelreichsten Gebiete der Erde. Etwa 30 Küstenvogelarten brüten mit über 100.000 Paaren im Nationalpark. Auch für viele Fischarten dient das Wattenmeer als „Kinderstube", darunter fallen wichtige Speisefischarten der Nordsee wie Scholle, Hering und Seezunge.

Das Gebiet des Nationalparks ist nach ökologischen Kriterien in zwei Schutzzonen gegliedert, welche Zugang und Schiffsverkehr räumlich und zeitlich, z.B. in der Vogelbrutzeit, regeln (s. Abb. 1).

Die Schutzzone 1, die dem stärksten Schutz unterliegt, darf im Gegensatz zur Schutzzone 2 grundsätzlich nicht betreten werden. Hier sind jedoch im Hinblick auf den Tourismus im küstennahen Watt Ausnahmen im Einvernehmen mit den betroffenen Gemeinden geschaffen worden, um das Wattwandern, Baden und Hobby-Fischen zu ermöglichen. Auch sind Ausnahmen im Rahmen festgelegter Routen, wie z.B. bei geführten Wattwanderungen (Abb. 3) möglich.

Abb. 3: Nationalpark-Wattführer mit Gruppe[3]

---

[3] Quelle: Nationalparkverwaltung Schleswig-Holsteinisches Wattenmeer, Gätje

3. Tourismus im Nationalpark und der Nationalparkregion

Die Nordseeküste ist ein traditionelles und beliebtes Urlaubsziel in Deutschland. Touristische Aktivitäten konzentrieren sich auf den Küstenstreifen und finden überwiegend am Strand oder Deich, auf dem bei Niedrigwasser trocken fallenden Watt bzw. am, im oder auf dem Wasser und in der küstennahen Landschaft statt.

Die Nationalpark-Region an der Westküste Schleswig-Holsteins verbuchte in 2006 knapp 1,84 Mio. Übernachtungsgäste mit 15 Mio. Übernachtungen (NBV 2006). Für das Jahr 2004 ermittelte das Tourismus-Barometer unter Einbeziehung des Grauen Beherbergungsmarktes (Verwandten- und Bekanntenbesuche, Freizeitwohnsitze) sogar eine Übernachtungszahl von 18,7 Mio. (Sparkassen- und Giroverband 2005). Der Anteil ausländischer Übernachtungsgäste beträgt seit Jahren nur 1-2 % (Sievers 2007). Zusätzlich zu den Übernachtungsgästen besuchten in 2006 rund 15 Millionen Tagesausflügler die Destination Nordsee Schleswig-Holstein (Maschke 2007).

Abb. 4: Wie stehen die Deutschen zu Nationalparks?[4]

---

[4] Quelle: Nationalparkverwaltung Schleswig-Holsteinisches Wattenmeer, Gätje

Dass Natur und Naturerlebnis eine ausschlaggebende Rolle bei der Wahl des Urlaubsortes spielen, lässt sich aus bundesweiten Repräsentativbefragungen eindeutig ermitteln. So stufen 8 von 10 deutschen Urlaubern „Natur erleben im Urlaub" als „wichtig" oder „besonders wichtig" ein (F.U.R 2007).

Bei einer deutschlandweiten Umfrage im Auftrag von EUROPARC, welche Rolle denn Nationalparks bei der Wahl des Urlaubsziels spielen würden, gaben 71 % der Befragten an, dass sie bevorzugt dort ihren Urlaub verbringen würden, wo man sich für den Schutz der Natur durch einen Nationalpark entschieden hätte (Abb. 4).[5] Dieses Ergebnis spiegelt das (steigende) Interesse an der Urlaubsreiseart ‚Natururlaub' und am Erleben von intakter Natur wieder, wofür Nationalparks eher als andere Destinationen als Garanten gelten dürften.

3.1 Voraussetzungen für einen nachhaltigen Tourismus im Nationalpark Schleswig-Holsteinisches Wattenmeer

„Der Mensch ist im Nationalpark ein willkommener Gast"[6], dieser Satz aus dem Leitbild des Nationalparks Schleswig-Holsteinisches Wattenmeer betont, dass Einheimische und Besucher keineswegs aus der Natur ausgeschlossen werden sollen. Im Gegenteil: Die Nationalparkverwaltung sorgt dafür, dass der Nationalpark Wattenmeer für die Menschen auf naturverträgliche Weise zugänglich und erlebbar ist, soweit es der Schutzzweck erlaubt. Im Nationalparkgesetz findet sich folgender Passus, der ausdrücklich auf die positiven Wirkungen des Naturschutzes auf den Tourismus und die regionale Bevölkerung Bezug nimmt:

„Der Erhalt der Natur durch den Nationalpark soll auch durch positive Rückwirkungen auf den Tourismus und das Ansehen der Region der nachhaltigen Entwicklung zur Verbesserung der Lebens- und Arbeitsbedingungen der im Umfeld lebenden Menschen dienen." (NPG, 1999, § 2 (3)).

Naturschutz und Tourismus müssen also nicht im Widerspruch zueinander stehen. Dennoch ist die Anwesenheit von Menschen in empfindlichen Naturgebieten immer mit Störungen verbunden. Um dem Schutzauftrag im Nationalpark gerecht zu werden und negative Auswirkungen

[5] Die Daten hat Dr. C. Kolmar, EUROPARC Deutschland, zur Verfügung gestellt.
[6] http://www.wattenmeer-nationalpark.de/ueber/unten4.htm

des Tourismus auf die Natur zu vermeiden oder wenigstens zu minimieren, wird im Nationalpark Schleswig-Holsteinisches Wattenmeer ein Bündel von Maßnahmen eingesetzt, die sich gegenseitig ergänzen:

- eine Zonierung des Gebietes (räumlich und/oder zeitlich),
- ein flächendeckendes System für Besucherinformation und Besucherlenkung,
- Einsatz von qualifiziertem und geschultem Personal vor Ort (Ranger, Naturschutzwarte, Nationalpark-WattführerInnen und MitarbeiterInnen von Naturschutzverbänden),
- ein vielfältiges und attraktives Naturerlebnis- und Bildungsangebot,
- regionale Zusammenarbeit mit den Tourismusorganisationen und touristischen Leistungsträgern.

Voraussetzung für den wirkungsvollen Einsatz dieser Maßnahmen ist eine gute Datengrundlage über die Verhältnisse im Nationalpark, z.b. über störungsempfindliche Bereiche wie Brut- und Mausergebiete oder Seehundliegeplätze. Diese Informationen liefert das Wattenmeer-Monitoring des Nationalparks, das Teil des trilateralen Monitoring-Programms der Wattenmeer-Anrainerländer Dänemark, Deutschland, Niederlande ist (CWSS 1999). Dabei werden u.a. Bestände von Vögeln, aber auch Störungen durch menschliche Eingriffe erfasst. Veränderungen können so zeitnah registriert und mögliche Konflikte gelöst werden (Gätje 2007, 45). Gästebefragungen im Rahmen des sozio-ökonomischen Monitorings geben darüber hinaus z.b. Informationen über die Akzeptanz von Schutzmaßnahmen und die Bekanntheit und Beliebtheit von Naturerlebnis-Angeboten.

Zonierung

Zonierung ist ein wirksames Instrument, um Raumkonflikte zwischen menschlicher Nutzung und störungsempfindlichen Pflanzen und Tieren zu lösen. In vielen Fällen sind zeitlich begrenzte Betretensverbote ausreichend, z.b. in Primärdünenbereichen während der Brutzeit von Seeregenpfeifer und Zwergseeschwalbe. Andere Bereiche wie z.b. die Vogelinsel Trischen sind aus Naturschutzgründen dauerhaft für den Zugang gesperrt. Der Schutz mausernder Brandgänse im Dithmarscher Wattenmeer wird über freiwillige Vereinbarungen mit Wassersportlern und Fischern erreicht.

Besucherlenkung und Besucherinformation

Ein wichtiges Instrument zur Umweltbildung und zum Schutz des Nationalparks stellt das Besucher-Informationssystem – kurz BIS – dar. Es vermittelt eine einheitliche Darstellung des Nationalparks, weist auf Naturerlebnismöglichkeiten innerhalb und außerhalb des Nationalparks hin. Der Nationalpark Schleswig-Holsteinisches Wattenmeer hat so eine attraktive Möglichkeit geschaffen, seine Besucher über die Küste, das Ökosystem und den Nationalpark zu informieren und gleichzeitig zu lenken.

Auf derzeit rund 115 Info-Tafeln (Abb. 5), 56 Info-Karten, 7 Naturpfaden, 1 Info-Wagen und 17 Info-Pavillons geben die BIS-Elemente unter dem Motto „Angebot statt Verbot" zahlreiche Tipps, wo und wie Natur genossen werden kann, aber auch was die Besucher zum Schutz und Erhalt des Nationalparks tun können (Nationalparkamt 2007, 14).

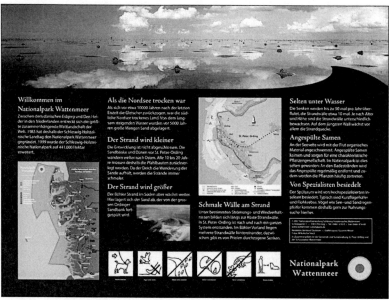

Abb. 5: Tafel des Besucher-Informationssystems (BIS)

Naturerlebnis und Bildung im Nationalpark

In der einzigartigen Landschaft des Nationalparks Wattenmeer gibt es eine Fülle von Möglichkeiten für intensives Natur-Erleben. Dabei erfreuen sich die nationalparkbezogenen Angebote großer Beliebtheit.

Sehr populär sind die geführten Wattwanderungen und -führungen, an denen in 2006 etwa 105.000 Menschen teilnahmen. Die rund 4.600 Wattveranstaltungen wurden zu über 70 % von MitarbeiterInnen (überwiegend junge Frauen im freiwilligen ökologischen Jahr und Zivildienstleistende) der Naturschutzverbände durchgeführt, größter Anbieter darunter war die Schutzstation Wattenmeer (Abb. 7). 25 % der Wattwanderungen wurden von zertifizierten Nationalpark-WattführerInnen organisiert. Die Naturschutzverbände und die Nationalpark-WattführerInnen sind wichtige Partner des Nationalparks für die Besucher-Information ebenso wie für das touristische und naturverträgliche Naturerleben und die Umweltbildung.

Abb. 6: Nationalpark-Ranger bei einer Schiffstour mit Seetierfang[7]

---

[7] Quelle: Nationalverwaltung Schleswig-Holsteinisches Wattenmeer, Ahlborn

Weitere Partner sind ausgewählte Reedereien, die in Kooperation mit dem Nationalpark von Rangern begleitete Schiffstouren im Nationalpark anbieten. Neben Fahrten zu den Seehundbänken werden auf vielen Touren auch Seetierfänge durchgeführt, bei denen ein Ranger die Tiere ausführlich und anschaulich erläutert. Dass diese Angebote bei einem breiten Publikum auf positive Resonanz stoßen, liegt einer nicht repräsentativen Umfrage nach vor allem daran, dass die Betreuung durch fachkompetentes Personal gewährleistet war. Für 79 % der Befragten war die Begleitung eines Nationalpark-Rangers ein wichtiges Entscheidungskriterium für die Fahrt.

Die Bedeutung einer kompetenten Betreuung durch geschultes Personal darf nicht unterschätzt werden. Eine umfangreiche Aus- und Fortbildung erhalten die Nationalpark-Ranger und die zertifizierten Nationalpark-WattführerInnen. Darüber hinaus werden die im Nationalpark eingesetzten MitarbeiterInnen der Naturschutzverbände (Abb. 7), die ehrenamtlichen Nationalpark-WartInnen und die Beschäftigten der Nationalpark-Partner-Betriebe über aktuellen Entwicklungen im Nationalpark informiert und zu speziellen Themen regelmäßig geschult.

Abb. 7: Salzwiesen-Exkursion mit der Schutzstation Wattenmeer[8]

---

[8] Quelle: Schutzstation Wattenmeer, Schulz

Als Alternative zum Strandbesuch stehen viele Indoor-Angebote für das Naturerleben zur Verfügung. Zahlreiche Info-Zentren des Nationalparks und der Naturschutzverbände informieren die Gäste mit Aquarien und interaktiven Ausstellungen über den Nationalpark Wattenmeer. Im Jahr 2006 besuchten 240.500 Gäste die Nationalpark-Infozentren in Tönning und Wyk auf Föhr sowie das Nationalpark-Haus in Husum, das in Kooperation mit dem WWF, der Schutzstation Wattenmeer und dem Kirchenkreis Husum-Bredstedt betrieben wird. Weitere 643.000 Gäste besuchten Ausstellungen der Naturschutzverbände und anderer Träger, die nur oder auch den Nationalpark Wattenmeer zum Gegenstand haben.

Das erfolgreichste Nationalpark-Zentrum ist das Multimar Wattforum in Tönning (Abb. 8). Seit seiner Eröffnung im Juni 1999 besuchten mehr als 1,7 Millionen Menschen die Ausstellung. Im Multimar Wattforum werden wissenschaftliche und biologische Zusammenhänge des Ökosystems Wattenmeer ansprechend und verständlich einer breiten Öffentlichkeit dargestellt. Das didaktische Konzept der Wissensvermittlung aus Entdecken und Erleben, Forschen und Spielen begeistert jung und alt. Das Multimar Wattforum stellt für die Region einen wesentlichen Wirtschaftsfaktor dar (Nationalparkamt 2007, 19).

Abb. 8: Walhaus im Multimar Wattforum[9]

---

[9] Quelle: Huppertz

Um den Besuchern der Region die Vielfalt von Naturerlebnisangeboten übersichtlich zu präsentieren und Informationen benutzerfreundlich anzubieten, hat die Nationalparkverwaltung in Kooperation mit der Nordsee-Tourismus-Service GmbH im Rahmen der Projekte „Natur & Tourismus" und LEADER+ „Naturerlebnis Wattenmeer im touristischen Angebot" die Internet-Plattform „Nordsee Naturerlebnis"[10] aufgebaut.

Interessierte Gäste oder auch MitarbeiterInnen von Tourist-Informationen können im sogenannten Naturerlebnisfinder Informationen über alle Naturerlebnisangebote, Termine und Anbieter in der gesamten Region finden. Die Grundlage für dieses umfassende Informationsangebot ist eine Datenbank, in der nach ausgewählten Kriterien zielgruppenorientierte Angebote herausgefiltert werden können.

Mit dem Informationssystem Naturerlebnis wird eine verbesserte Nutzung des naturtouristischen Potenzials der Nordseeküste Schleswig-Holsteins im touristischen Marketing erreicht.

3.2 Nationalpark-Partnerschaften

Nationalpark-Partnerschaften sind Kooperationen zwischen dem Nationalparkamt und touristischen Betrieben oder Kommunen in der Nationalparkregion. Die gemeinsamen Ziele dieser Zusammenarbeit beziehen sich vorrangig auf den Schutz des schleswig-holsteinischen Wattenmeeres und die Förderung des nachhaltigen Tourismus (s. Abb. 9).

Der Titel und das Logo „Nationalpark-Partner" wird durch einen Vergaberat, in dem Nationalpark und Kommunalpolitik, Naturschutzverbände, die Nationalpark-Wattführer und die Nordsee-Tourismus-Service GmbH vertreten sind, an Unternehmen vergeben, die nationalparkbezogene Kriterien und grundlegende Umweltstandards nach Viabono[11] erfüllen.

Mit der Kooperations-Vereinbarung verpflichten sich die Unternehmen zur Einhaltung dieser Umweltstandards, die Ziele und Leitgedanken des Nationalparks zu unterstützen, an regelmäßigen Fortbildungsveranstaltungen teilzunehmen und einen Kostenbeitrag zu entrichten. Die Nationalpark-Partner profitieren im Gegenzug von der Nutzung des Natio-

---

[10] http://www.nordsee-naturerlebnis.de
[11] Viabono ist die deutsche Umweltdachmarke für touristische Produkte, http://www.viabono.de/

nalpark-Logos (Abb. 10), von zur Verfügung gestellten Informationsmaterial und einem umfassenden Cross-Marketing durch die Partnerschaft.

Ziele der Nationalpark-Partnerschaft

Identifizierung mit den Zielen und Leitsätzen des Nationalparks

Gegenseitige Wertschätzung und Respekt

Erhaltung und Schutz des Schleswig-Holsteinischen Wattenmeeres

Enge Zusammenarbeit und Kommunikation, Vernetzung

Gemeinsam für den Nationalpark

Sensibilisierung und Information der Gäste

Nutzung für das Außen- und Innen-Marketing

Schaffung eines Benefits für die Partner und eines Mehrwerts für den Gast

Instrument zur Stärkung qualitativ besonders hochwertiger und nachhaltiger Tourismusangebote

Abb. 9: Ziele der Nationalpark-Partnerschaft[12]

Das Nationalpark-Partnerprojekt in Schleswig-Holstein übernimmt eine Vorbildfunktion für regionale Kooperationen, an denen sich inzwischen weitere deutsche Nationalparks orientieren.[13] Es ist ein positives Beispiel wie Tourismus und Naturschutz voneinander profitieren können. Bislang gibt es in Schleswig-Holstein 60 zertifizierte Nationalpark-Partner zu denen 5 Reedereien, 3 Hotels, 4 Ferienwohnungsvermieter, 2 Restaurants, 2 Gemeinden, 1 Eisenbahngesellschaft, 1 Reiseveranstalter und 42 WattführerInnen zählen. Urlauber und Tagesgäste profitieren von kompetenter Information, qualitativ hochwertigen Angeboten, die umweltfreundlich sind und attraktive Naturerlebnisse bieten.

---

[12] Quelle: Nationalparkverwaltung Schleswig-Holsteinisches Wattenmeer
[13] http://www.nationalpark-partner.de/

Abb. 10: Frisch gebackene Nationalpark-Partner von Hallig Hooge

3.3 Der Nationalpark als regionaler Wirtschaftsfaktor

Der Tourismus ist einer der wichtigsten Wirtschaftsfaktoren für die Region des schleswig-holsteinischen Wattenmeeres. Er trägt mit 37,5 % zum Volkseinkommen bei (Nordseebäderverband 2006, 16).

Inwiefern der Nationalpark-Tourismus Anteil an der regionalen Wertschöpfung hat, war erstmals Grundlage einer wirtschaftswissenschaftlichen Untersuchung in 2003. Diese erfolgte im Rahmen einer Diplomarbeit (Korff 2004) an der Technischen Universität Dresden in Zusammenarbeit mit der inspektour GmbH[14], der Fachhochschule Westküste und der Nationalparkverwaltung.

Rund 1.100 Übernachtungs- und Tagesgäste der Region wurde gefragt, welche Rolle der Nationalpark bei ihrer Reisezielentscheidung spielte. Für 25 % der Übernachtungsgäste spielte der Nationalpark eine

---

[14] Institut für praxisorientierte Entwicklung & Konzepte im Tourismus/Kooperationspartner der Fachhochschule Westküste

wichtige Rolle bei der Wahl des Reiseziels. Diese Gruppe kann in einem weiteren Sinne als Nationalpark-Touristen gedeutet werden.

Für einen kleinen Prozentsatz von 1,4 % war der Nationalpark sogar das Hauptentscheidungskriterium für einen Aufenthalt in der Region. Für diese relativ kleine Gruppe von Nationalparkgästen im engeren Sinne, lässt sich, unter Hinzuziehung weiterer statistischer Daten zum regionalen Tourismus, eine Bruttowertschöpfung von 6,4 Millionen Euro hochrechnen. Das entspricht 280 Vollzeitarbeitsplätzen.

Die größere Gruppe der Nationalpark-Touristen im weiteren Sinne, für die der Nationalpark eine wichtige Rolle bei der Urlaubsentscheidung spielte, steht für eine Wertschöpfung von 131 Millionen Euro oder 5.900 Arbeitsplätze (Korff 2004).

Damit spielt der Nationalpark-Tourismus eine bedeutende Rolle in der regionalen Wirtschaft und in der Verbesserung der touristischen Infrastruktur. Die Region profitiert nicht nur wirtschaftlich vom Nationalpark, sie gewinnt auch an Image und Attraktivität – ein Vorteil im Wettbewerb zu anderen Regionen. Eine stärkere Präsenz des Nationalparks in der touristischen Vermarktung, die Weiterentwicklung von naturbezogenen Angeboten sowie eine stärkere Identifizierung der regionalen Bevölkerung mit dem Nationalpark können diese Effekte noch verstärken.

3.4 Das Sozio-ökonomische Monitoring im Nationalpark

Die Erfassung rein ökologischer Daten erlaubt keinen Einblick in Trends und Entwicklungen, die sich im sozialen und wirtschaftlichen, speziell im touristischen Sektor in der Wattenmeerregion ankündigen. Gerade im nachhaltigen Tourismus sind das Verhalten und die Meinung der Gäste im Hinblick auf die Natur und den Naturschutz sehr wichtig, um Lenkungs- und Aufklärungsmaßnahmen effizient und dabei auch akzepabel gestalten zu können. Ebenso von Bedeutung ist der Blick auf die regionale Wirtschaft und auf die Perzeption und Akzeptanz der Bevölkerung gegenüber dem Vorgehen der Schutzgebietsverwaltung (vgl. Gätje 2007, 45).

Die sozio-ökonomische Datenerhebung ist auch unabdingbar für die im Leitlinien von EUROPARC Deutschland bzw. im Nationalpark-Gesetz formulierten sozio-ökonomischen Ziele (Gätje 2003, 246), u.a.:

- Positive Rückwirkung des Schutzgebietes auf den Tourismus und das Ansehen der Region,
- Förderung eines naturverbundenen Tourismus,
- Erhöhung der Nachfrage nach regionalen Angeboten,
- Einbeziehung der regionalen Bewohner bei Planungen und Maßnahmen,
- Stärkere Identifizierung der Bevölkerung mit dem Schutzgebiet,
- Bereitstellung exemplarischer Erkenntnisse über die Wechselwirkungen von natürlichen und gesellschaftlichen Prozessen, von wirtschaftlicher Nutzung und der Entwicklung von natürlichen Lebensräumen.

Der erste Entwurf für ein sozio-ökonomisches Monitoring im Nationalpark Schleswig-Holsteinisches Wattenmeer, das „SÖM Watt", wurde 1997 in Kooperation mit dem Deutschen Wirtschaftswissenschaftlichen Institut für Fremdenverkehr an der Universität München (dwif) erstellt. (Möller & Feil 1997) Die Nationalparkverwaltung entwickelte diese Konzeption weiter und begann 1999 mit ihrer Umsetzung. Das „SÖM-Watt" ist Teil des Trilateralen Wattenmeer-Monitoring (TMAP) (Landesamt für den Nationalpark Schleswig-Holsteinisches Wattenmeer 2001) (Gätje 2007, 46).

Das „SÖM-Watt" besteht aus drei Komponenten (s. Abb. 11). Das „SÖM Regional" umfasst ausgewählte Daten aus eigenen und amtlichen Statistiken, z.B. über die regionale Tourismusentwicklung (Übernachtungs-und Gästezahlen, Aufenthaltsdauer). Dokumentiert werden auch Erhebungen aus Einzeluntersuchungen zu wirtschaftlichen Aspekten in der Nationalparkregion (z.B. Korff 2004), Teilnehmerzahlen bei Wattführungen und Besucherzahlen in Infozentren.

Im „SÖM Trend" (seit 1999) werden die Angaben aus Gästebefragungen von Touristen und Tagesausflüglern zusammengefasst, die die Rangerinnen und Ranger des Nationalparks im Auftrag der Nationalparkverwaltung durchführen. Die Befragungen finden an 14 Tagen im Jahr (je vier Tage im Frühjahr und Herbst und sechs Tage im Sommer) an insgesamt 16 ausgewählten Standorten statt. Hinzu kommen die Daten aus zeitgleich durchgeführten Gästezählungen und Kurzbefragungen zur Besucherzahl und -struktur.

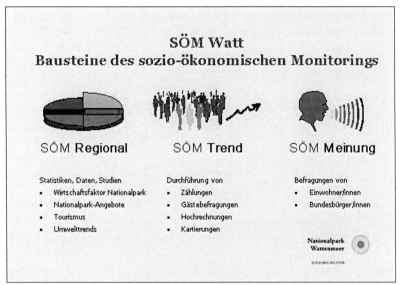

Abb. 11: Die drei Bausteine des SÖM Watt[15]

Die „SÖM Meinung" lässt Aufschluss über den Bekanntheitsgrad, Wahrnehmung und Akzeptanz des Nationalparks in der regionalen Bevölkerung zu. Grundlage bilden die jährlichen Telefonbefragungen der inspektour GmbH im Auftrag der Nationalparkverwaltung, bestehend aus einer repräsentativen Stichprobe von 600 Einwohnerinnen und Einwohnern aus den an den Nationalpark angrenzenden Landkreisen Nordfriesland und Dithmarschen (Gätje 2007, 46-48).

Die Haltung der Bevölkerung zum Nationalpark ist überaus positiv. Auf die Frage, wie bedeutsam es für sie sei, einen Nationalpark vor der Tür zu haben, wählten 35 % die Antwortmöglichkeit „Darauf können wir stolz sein" aus (Abb. 12). Weitere 53 % antworteten, es sei ihnen wichtig. Für eine negative Aussage entschieden sich nur 3 % der Befragten.

---

[15] Quelle: Nationalparkverwaltung Schleswig-Holsteinisches Wattenmeer

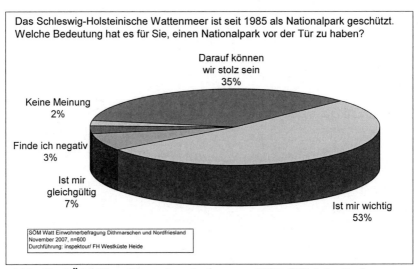

Das Schleswig-Holsteinische Wattenmeer ist seit 1985 als Nationalpark geschützt.
Welche Bedeutung hat es für Sie, einen Nationalpark vor der Tür zu haben?

Darauf können
wir stolz sein
35%

Keine Meinung
2%

Finde ich negativ
3%

Ist mir
gleichgültig
7%

Ist mir wichtig
53%

SÖM Watt Einwohnerbefragung Dithmarschen und Nordfriesland
November 2007, n=600
Durchführung: inspektour/ FH Westküste Heide

**Abb. 12: SÖM Watt Einwohnerbefragung 2007: "Welche Bedeutung
hat es für Sie, einen Nationalpark vor der Tür zu haben?"** [16]

Der Nutzen des „SÖM Watt" zeigt sich in der Möglichkeit zur raschen
Wahrnehmung von Veränderungen und Trends. So können Informati-
ons-und Naturerlebnisangebote und Schutzmaßnahmen zeitnah opti-
miert werden. Die Bedeutung des Nationalparks für die wirtschaftliche
und touristische Entwicklung wird ermittelt und bietet politische Argu-
mentationshilfe. Auch die Meinungen und Interessen von Touristen und
Einheimischen können besser berücksichtigt werden, um mehr Akzeptanz gegenüber dem Schutzgebiet zu schaffen.

4. Fazit

Naturschutz und Tourismus sind sehr wohl in der Lage, Hand in Hand
zusammen zu arbeiten. Die Kooperation zwischen Nationalpark und
Tourismus in Schleswig-Holstein ist ein gelungenes Beispiel für eine
vielversprechende, aber noch ausbaufähige Entwicklung zum nachhaltigen Tourismus. Die intensive, konstruktive Zusammenarbeit zwischen
Tourismus und Nationalpark sorgt für positive Effekte in ökonomi-

---

[16] Quelle: inspektour GmbH, Fachhochschule Westküste/Heide Holstein

schen, sozialen und ökologischen Bereichen, z.B. durch die Sicherung und Schaffung von Arbeitsplätzen, die Vermittlung von authentischem Naturerlebnis, die Steigerung des Bildungsgrades in der Bevölkerung und damit die Zunahme des Verständnisses für Naturschutzmaßnahmen (Trimborn 2007, 89).

Die Schleswig-Holsteinische Westküste ist und bleibt mit ihrem Naturpotenzial eines der wichtigsten Reiseziele in Deutschland. Die zunehmende Nachfrage nach Natururlaub und nationalparktouristischen Angeboten in den letzten Jahren spiegelt das steigende Interesse der Menschen an intakter Umwelt, am Besuch von Naturattraktionen und authentischem Naturgenuß im Urlaub wider. Der Nationalpark und die hiesige Tourismuswirtschaft sind aufgefordert, ihre Kooperationen zu festigen, zu intensivieren und zu erweitern, um dieser Nachfrage gerecht zu werden.

Christiane Gätje & Maren Babinsky

Literaturverzeichnis

BNatSchG: *Bundesnaturschutzgesetz vom 25.03.2002*. Zuletzt geändert am 09.12.2006

BMU & EUROPARC (2007): *Pressemitteilung der Parlamentarischen Staatssekretärin im Bundesumweltministerium Astrid Klug und EUROPARC Deutschland e.V.* http://www.bmu.de/pressemitteilungen/aktuelle_pressemitteilungen/pm/38824.php

CWSS (Hg.) (1998): *Ministerial Declaration of the Eighth Trilateral Governmental Conference on the Protection of the Wadden Sea*. Stade, Germany, October 22, 1997.

EUROPARC (Hg.) (2005): *Deutsche Nationalparks, Naturparks und Biosphärenreservate. Leitbilder.* Berlin. http://www.europarc-deutschland.de/dateien/bilder/Leitbilder.pdf

F.U.R (Forschungsgemeinschaft Urlaub und Reisen e.V.) (Hg.) (2007): *Die 37. Reiseanalyse RA 2007*. Kiel.

Gätje, Christiane (2003): *Sozio-ökonomisches Monitoring der schleswig-holsteinischen Wattenmeerregion.* In: Deutsches MAB-Nationalkomitee beim Bundesministerium für Umwelt, Naturschutz und Reaktorsicherheit (Hg.): *Voller Leben. UNESCO-Biosphärenreservate-Modellregionen für eine Nachhaltige Entwicklung*. Bonn. 245-250.

Gätje, Christiane (2007): *Das sozio-ökonomische Monitoring im Nationalpark Schleswig-Holsteinisches Wattenmeer.* In: Biosphärenreservat Vessertal-Thüringer Wald (Hg.): *Besuchermonitoring und ökonomische Effekte in Nationalen Naturlandschaften.* Schmiedefeld am Rennsteig. 44-49

Korff, Katja (2004): *Die regionalwirtschaftliche Bedeutung des nationalparkorientierten Übernachtungstourismus am Schleswig-Holsteinischen Wattenmeer. Diplomarbeit Technische Universität Dresden.*

Landesamt für den Nationalpark Schleswig-Holsteinisches Wattenmeer (Hg.) (2001): *Wattenmeermonitoring 2000.* Tönning.*(= Schriftenreihe des Nationalparks Schleswig-Holsteinisches Wattenmeer, Sonderheft)*

Landesamt für den Nationalpark Schleswig-Holsteinisches Wattenmeer (Hg.) (2007): *Erfolgreiche Kooperation für Mensch und Natur. Nationalpark und Tourismus.* Broschüre. Tönning.

Landesamt für den Nationalpark Schleswig-Holsteinisches Wattenmeer (Hg.) (2007): *Meeresgrund trifft Horizont.* Broschüre. Tönning.

Maschke, J. (2007): (Hg.): *Tagesreisen der Deutschen Teil III*, Schriftenreihe 52 (122 S.). dwif München.

Möller, A. & Feil, T. (1997): Konzept Sozioökonomisches Monitoring im National-park *Schleswig-Holsteinisches Wattenmeer.* Unveröffentl. Bericht. München/Berlin/Tönning.

NPG (1999): *Gesetz zum Schutz des schleswig-holsteinischen Wattenmeeres vom 24.10.1996.* Zuletzt geändert am 17.12.1999.

Nordseebäderverband Schleswig-Holstein e.V. (Hg.) (2006): *Mehrwert. Die Bedeutung des Tourismus für die Region und warum wir alle davon profitieren. Zahlen. Daten. Fakten.* Kiel.

Nordseebäderverband Schleswig-Holstein e.V. (2007): *Tourismusstatistik 2006.* Husum.

Sievers, T. (2007): *Studie zur (potentiellen) Bedeutung ausländischer Touristen am Schleswig-Holsteinischen Wattenmeer.* Unveröffentl. Bericht im Auftrag des Nationalparkamtes. Inspektour, Heide.

Sparkassen- und Giroverband für Schleswig-Holstein (Hg.) (2005): *Tourismusbarometer Jahresbericht 2005 – Management Summary Schleswig-Holstein.* Kiel.

Trimborn, Ralf (2007): *Nationalpark Schleswig-Holsteinisches Wattenmeer als regionaler Wirtschaftsfaktor.* In: Biosphärenreservat Vessertal-Thüringer Wald (Hg.): *Besuchermonitoring und ökonomische Effekte in Nationalen Naturlandschaften.* Schmiedefeld am Rennsteig. 86-90

National Park Tourism in Germany: The Economic Perspective[1]

Manuel Woltering

Abstract

In Germany nature based tourism and ecotourism play a subordinate role in incoming and domestic tourism alike, whereas in outgoing tourism the ecotourism segment makes up a larger proportion. Internationally, protected areas and especially the most famous group of national parks have been considered major tourist attractions for quite some time. This coincides with an international trend in environmental politics to increasingly foreground the regional economic effects protected areas can generate as a result their contribution to regional economic development in peripheral and structurally disadvantaged regions where national parks are typically located. In Germany though, national parks are only recently attracting attention in the tourism industry. Also regional politics has just started to be more attentive to the economic impacts of protected areas.

The results of the following research clearly indicate that tourism in national parks can generate considerable benefits for the regional economy. For instance, in Mueritz National Park it is estimated that guests whose key motivation for visiting was the brand 'National Park' (a share of nearly 44% of all 390,000 visitors in 2004) created an amount of 261 income equivalents. In National Park Berchtesgaden only about 10% of 1.13 million visitors in 2002 can be classified as national park tourist in a strict sense, generating about 206 income equivalents.

As indicated by the research findings, more importance should be attached to the issue of tourism in protected areas. Financial benefits of tourism in national parks may contribute to increasing acceptance of nature conservation. Therefore decision-making processes in nature protection and regional tourism policy need to more fully incorporate aspects of durable economic development.

---

[1] A draft version of this paper was presented at the Tourism & Hospitality Research Conference "Beyond Nature" in Dunedin, New Zealand by Hartmann, Job and Metzler in December 2006.

1. Introduction

What kinds of regional economic benefits can tourism induce in national parks and other protected areas? This is the main question of this contribution.

Even though the IUCN figures on protected areas – nearly 13% of the terrestrial area of our planet is formally protected at present (IUCN 2005) – might suggest a different conclusion, setting aside territory for the mere purpose of preservation has proven difficult, especially in developing countries with population growth resulting in extension of agricultural frontiers, increasing needs for land to live and the consumption of other natural resources. Yet, not only in such countries have acceptance problems arisen. As being no-go areas for many uses, national parks frequently lack a good reputation within local communities in industrialized countries, too. Therefore economic rationale moved into the centre of attention in order to justify conservationist's activities to protect certain natural landscapes of intrinsic value. At this point it is tourism which generates financial benefits through visiting of those protected areas (Walpole et al. 2001).

Designating national parks usually means to abandon other utilizations. This results in the controversially discussed issue if and how the formerly existent added value – e.g. through forestry – can be compensated? Consequently the question must be raised which regional economic benefits a national park may induce? The regional economic impacts on local communities as a result of tourism are of particular importance, although they cannot be covered sufficiently because of data generating problems. So far this topic has been the focal point of interest of only a few research studies in Central Europe (Schmidt 2006; Job et al. 2005, Job et al. 2003; Küpfer 2000) which can hardly be compared because of their different methodological approaches. As part of a comprehensive survey national park visitation was closely monitored and interviews were conducted with visitors particularly with regard to tourist spending. The target was to generate a standardized procedure for estimating the economic benefits of tourism in protected areas of Germany.

This contribution is structured as follows: First of all section II deals with the overall situation of national parks in Germany. Then section III discusses the relationship between national parks and tourism, while section IV explains the regional economic aspects of national park tourism; section V introduces the method used for estimating the economic impacts and section VI then shows the results of two case studies. Section VII discusses the outcomes and finally gives some reasoning for future research.

2.   National Parks in Germany

In Germany the size of the 14 national parks ranges from 3,000 up to nearly 450,000 ha (including water area and tidelands), covering only less than 1% of terrestrial territory. Their share of the strictly protected core zone varies considerably between 10.7 and 91.5%. German national parks are relatively young. Being the prototype, in Bavarian Forest the idea to implement a national park was realized in 1970 only; Eifel and Kellerwald-Edersee were proclaimed in 2004. As figure 1 shows, Germany's national parks are mainly located in peripheral regions with low population density and economic power, either squeezed to the country's borders or located in remote highlands (Job 2008).

When looking at the management of national parks and trying to compare national to international levels, important differences are obvious. As defined by German environmental law IUCN criteria differ from national parks targets. In both cases the protection of nature, ecosystems and resources is of central importance. On an international level though, tourism and recreation are stressed as a main aim: "protected area management [is] mainly for ecosystem protection and recreation" (IUCN 2003). This is not the case in Germany, where the subordinate targets "environmental education" and "experience of nature" are stressed instead. Recreational use is of minor importance (BNatSchG 2002, §24). This contrasts to the status of national parks e.g. in New Zealand where they are the main pull factor for incoming tourism as "...places that have been set aside for their intrinsic worth and for the benefit, use and enjoyment of the public..." (DOC 2005). The emphasis is given to tourism in this context which points to the backward development and inferior status that is still ascribed to national park tourism in Germany.

"Nationale Naturlandschaften" is the latest marketing activity, promoting all 14 national parks, 14 biosphere reserves, and 95 nature parks in Germany. This umbrella brand should help to boost popularity and attractiveness of these areas. The efforts have been fruitful, as 20

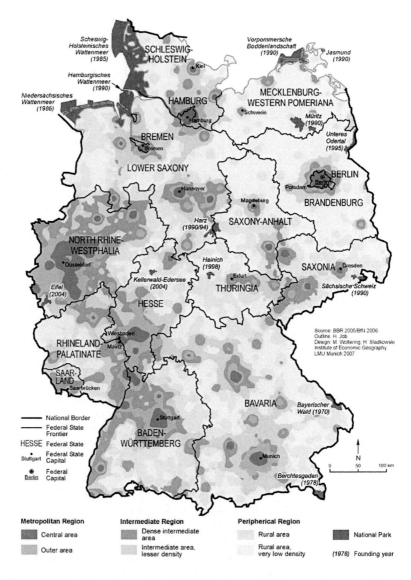

Fig. 1: National parks and spatial structure of Germany

million visitors have already been counted, or rather estimated to have been through German national parks (VDN 2006).

3. National Parks and Tourism

The term national park has a positive connotation in tourism. It signifies authentic natural experiences and therefore represents one of the most important objectives of travel, according to future trends in tourism. During the last few decades the number of protected areas as well as the recreational use of national parks has increased. Today in many countries national parks serve as major attractions in nature-based tourism and the visitation of reserves will continue to rise (Strasdas 2007).

Internationally, protected areas have been considered major tourist attractions for quite some time. The recently published World Conservation Union (IUCN) list of protected areas states that there are approximately 113,700 protected areas covering roughly 13% of the global land mass; marine protected areas are not included (IUCN 2005). Especially during the second half of the last century the total number and area classified under the six categories of protected areas increased exponentially, leaving protected areas really en vogue today. Undoubtedly quite a few of those protected areas exist as mere "paper parks" without adequate protection measures. This holds especially true for marine protected areas, where many parks exist on maps but no effort to protect the resources and ecosystems is undertaken. These "paper parks" are declared as protected areas and then left alone with insufficient management activities and a lack of funding destining them to degradation (Del Valle 2002). Nevertheless a huge number of protected areas exist, where a successful coexistence of protection and tourism activities is to be observed, frequently protected areas being major national destinations of tourism.

The actual situation in Germany can be specified as follows: A market analysis carried out in 2004 states that experiencing nature as a means of motivation for travel and choosing a destination is of major importance for 67% of German tourists. In 2005, those figures increased further to 79% (DTV 2005). Also visiting natural attractions frequently or very frequently during the holiday is decisive for about 45%. But in spite of these very positive figures, there are just a few people, whose sole purpose of the trip was indicated as nature-related – they make up only

7% of all holidaymakers. In 2005, a total of 64.1 million trips (of 5 days or more) have been counted, opening an immense market potential for nature tourism, though main destinations are still to be found in Europe and the Mediterranean, where 95% of all trips of Germans lead (Strasdas 2004).

Research conducted by other institutions arrived at similar conclusions. In compliance with DTV (2005) the chance to visit national parks, or respectively protected areas during a trip, is crucial for the travel decision for around a third of German tourists. However, only a mere 6% actually visit a national park or another type of large scale protected area during their holiday. Interestingly, of all nature related trips, 51% led to destinations outside of Germany. Only 31% of all trips remained within the country, strongly indicating the great prominence of outgoing tourism (DTV 2005). Therefore it is not surprising that Germany, as well as the United Kingdom in Europe, North America, Australia and New Zealand account for the main sources of tourists for nature tourism to developing countries (Strasdas 2001). Furthermore, incoming tourism is of marginal relevance: 82% of all arrivals in Germany in 2005 were domestic and the remaining 18% of arrivals mainly travel on sight seeing trips of the main cities, leaving protected areas very much aside.

4. National Parks and their Regional Economic Significance

If taken into account that national parks bear different values, particularly ecological functions like carbon sequestration or watershed protection, they can be seen as public goods. Most values show properties of non-rivalry and non-excludability. The values of national parks can be enjoyed commonly without disturbing any other individual's consumption of that good (Samuelson 1954). Accordingly, consumers cannot be excluded from the usage of values provided by national parks. Furthermore there does not exist any process of price-building in the market for these goods as it is common for private goods (e.g. clothing, furniture). Hence it is difficult to determine the total economic value of a national park as a public good.

Economic values of protected areas comprise different components: use values and non-use values (Pearce/Turner 1990). The non-use values can be further distinguished in three different types of values: The so-called existence values are closely associated with the intrinsic significance of nature. They reflect the benefit of knowing that the protected area exists even though the probability of visiting it or getting direct use of it in another way is quite low. Rather similar are the intentions of the bequest values which refer to the will of some people to protect e.g. special natural phenomena for future generations. At last the option values are also related to the future possibilities of using protected areas respectively their resources, e.g. because of its biodiversity as an untested gene pool for pharmaceutical or agricultural products (WCPA 1998). Within the other category of use values a distinction has to be made between direct and indirect ones: While the latter comprise primarily ecological functions like e.g. avalanche or watershed protection, which are usually not measured by any market, the former are of particular interest for a local economy. Amongst others they include activities such as agriculture, forestry, hunting, but also recreation and tourism – values derived from the direct use of national parks.

De facto, in most protected areas the only permitted economic form of usage is tourism. In general the relationship between nature conservation and tourism can be seen as ambivalent: On the one hand tourism is often based on a sound environment, whereas on the other side unmanaged tourism may affect natural processes adversely. In spite of the numerous drawbacks, tourism can also have some positive effects on the nature. Focusing on the local population missing acceptance for the goals of nature conservation often can be found. Many inhabitants of buffer zones of protected areas feel that they are restricted in their private, but also job-related actions through the conservation restrictions. Positive economic impacts and possibilities to participate in tourism-related jobs and income help to show that regions with protected areas do not necessarily end up as black holes of economic development. Therefore tourism represents an opportunity to conserve endangered ecosystems while it may also has positive effects on regional development. Because of their mostly peripheral position it is thought about protected areas as a conscious instrument for sustainable development, even in Central Europe (e.g. Hammer 2003). For this reason the main emphasis of regional studies on the impacts of tourism are their effects on income and employment.

5. Measuring effects of national parks in regional economies

5.1 Data generation

In all studies on economic impacts of national parks the main information needed is tourism demand or in other words turnover originating from expenditures of park visitors. Different forms of data gathering have been tested, which potentially comprise oral interviews (face-to-face or telephone) making up the category of recall interview methods. These can be opposed to written forms or diary techniques, where expenditures are noted in fixed time intervals or directly after the expense was made. Faulkner and Raybould (1995) tested different techniques, resulting in significant variations, namely lower estimates in recall interviews compared to diary methods. The findings indicate that a memory decay effect may be apparent. Breen et al. (2001) confirm these results and point out that additional behavioural influences, especially peer pressure may also lead to biased results. Therefore the setting of the interviews (individual vs. individual in group) needs to be considered. Even though diary methods may seem preferable they may suffer of response bias (selection effects), especially when the diaries have to be sent back by the interviewee.

In all forms, expenditures are surveyed in categories. Usually, the number and content of the categories is set up to match further impact analysis calculations, but influences of the empirical design on the results are highly conceivable. Yuan and Yuan (1996) therefore tested different numbers of expenditure categories. They found that tradeoffs between the data detail and interview length have to be considered. Whereas a certain number of categories is needed for the impact assessment, longer interviews may reduce interviewee attention resulting in less accurate data or even interviewees leaving interviews early. In this sense it may be argued in favour of a reduced number of categories.

From the empirical data usually mean daily expenditures are derived. In order to obtain the entire tourism demand, the daily figures are multiplied by the aggregated days that visitors spend in the area. To take out some of the variation in the mean daily budgets different tourist groups are distinguished, like day trippers or overnight guests. For such calculations reliable visitor data is needed. Especially in parks where no entrance fees are charged in most cases neither counting nor book keeping of visitors is implemented. Data on visitors are often rough estimates with information on different visitor groups completely absent, like in Germany (Job 2008).

5.2 The model

A main step in economic impact analysis is to model the regional economy in order to give estimations of the magnitude of the impact. Figure 2 displays that the expenditures of tourists are seen as external injections into the regional finance flows, setting into action economic processes over different rounds. This process causes so-called multiplier effects, meaning that income originating from tourist expenditures not only benefits enterprises and workers directly receiving the expenses, but also showing indirect and induced income effects in supplying enterprises. Altogether the direct, indirect and induced effects result in a

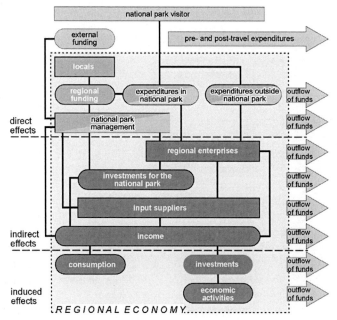

Fig. 2: National parks and regional economics[2]

---

[2] Job/Metzler 2006; cf. Metzler 2007

higher total income than in the initial round. The multiplier expresses the ratio of direct to indirect and induced income (Archer 1984). Value-added studies concentrate on the first round (direct) effects. In focus is the added value, which is defined as the amount of turnover that is used as wages and earnings. This means that supply-side studies are necessary or third-party data is used that deliver the share of wages and earnings in relation to turnover in the relevant sectors in which tourist expenditures may occur. The effects of tourism on the Swiss National Park were estimated using this method. Küpfer (2000) uses data of a previous study for the added value quote and calculates a gross added-value of US$, 7.7 million translating into 120 full-time job equivalents (FTE).

When it comes to evaluating the effects of tourism in most cases Input-Output-Analysis is used as a model for the economy (Fletcher 1989). On the basis of transaction matrices, linkages between different sectors of the economy in question (local, regional or national) are analysed. These tables show how much input one sector needs from other sectors to produce a certain output, so that estimates can be given what impact additional demand in one sector has on the whole economy (figure 2). Together with algebra of matrices different types of multipliers and effects on incomes can be calculated. On the basis of an Input-Output model Mules (2004) calculates for his case study of Kosciuszko National Park (Australia) an impact of around US$ 120 million of gross state product. This gross state product consciously excludes expenditures of tourists from the same state and is responsible for 2,300 jobs, expressed in FTE terms.

Thorbecke (1985) advocates Social Accounting Matrices (SAM) that share common features with Input-Output-Analysis but are an extended framework. In general models of this type calculate a positive effect for any increase in economic activity, even though e.g. resource-restrictions might cutoff supply. Strict assumptions of Input-Output-Analysis have to be made responsible for such unwanted results. A SAM-based case study was done in Área de Proteção Ambiental de Guaraqueçaba (Brazil). There an economic effect of 19,425 US$ in wage payment or 32 FTE is derived from tourists expenditures (Wagner 1997).

An even more sophisticated way of measuring impacts of tourism are Computable General Equilibrium (CGE) models. Dwyer et al. (2004) prefer CGE calculation over Input-Output models because other markets can be captured and feedback effects may be incorporated. Such effects occur because mobilizing resources like workers or finances diverts them from other uses that might be more beneficial. Especially in national studies price effects due to a strong demand of the national currency by foreign tourists occur, showing impacts on import and export industries. In a nutshell, changes in tourism demand lead to changes in economic patterns, so that e.g. the linear production function that is assumed when Input-Output-Analysis is used is not fixed. Drawbacks of CGE are the complexity and data needed to build the models, making CGE comparatively costly. Particularly for the regional level Dwyer at al. (2004) acknowledge that the expenses for building such a model may well not be justified. This is underlined by the fact that different shortcomings which CGE models circumvent do not have great influence at this scale, e.g. regional economies are quite open for factor flows.

Even though both techniques, SAM and Input-Output-Analysis, can be set up with much lower efforts than CGE models, great input is necessary. Complexity is aggravated when basic data is incomplete or missing, which is often the case on a regional level. To help out, regional Input-Output tables are then derived from national tables, which are adopted via Location Quotients (Brandt et al. 2001). Doing so increases the number of assumptions on which Input-Output models are based, which leads to decreased reliability of the results. Referring to that Patriquin et al. (2002) are discussing an alternative, hybrid approach of impact measurement by SAM. This involves the collection of park-specific data therefore promising greater accuracy and validity as crude top down Input-Output models (like the well known US 'IMPLAN').

Because of missing regional data for an accurate Input-Output analysis in Central Europe up to now the impacts of national parks have been assessed on the basis of gathering data on a bottom-up scale only. The focus of the following case study will be on this issue, i.e. on the direct use values and especially the economic effects created by tourism investigated in terms of a value-added-analysis in two German national parks: Mueritz National Park and National Park Berchtesgaden.

5.3 Methodology

In short, when it comes to evaluating economic impacts of protected areas, three data pools are necessary:

1. data on visitor numbers in different categories (day trippers, overnight visitors),
2. expenditure data and
3. a model for multiplier estimation.

Building up all three data sets can be very expensive and may well exceed cost and time budgets for the evaluation. Hence, it is reasonable to seek for alternative data sources. For the multiplier estimation there is a clear consensus that multiplier should not be transferred to other regions as they depend very much on regional economic structures in all probability not existent in others. Therefore sound project-specific calculation of the multipliers is an absolute must. On the other hand extensive primary surveys can be avoided if third party data is available for expenditures and visitors. Nevertheless, using such data has drawbacks. One critical factor of the research is the total number of guests visiting the parks.

Because no trustworthy figures on numbers existed in the National Park Berchtesgaden study figures for visitor numbers was estimated through data from electronic parking meters that logged ticket type and the exact date of ticket emission. Such an approach seems to be reasonable as most of the visitors have to use a car to get to the mainly remote starting places for trails in the park which is situated in a natural dead end-situation (Job et al. 2003). For the calculation of economic effects, we control for multiple visits to the national park by the same visitor. The parking meter data also allowed gathering information on spatial and temporal distribution of the visits, helping to improve the sampling of visitors. The data on the role of the national park in the destination decision process, and expenditure data, was collected with intercept interviews (1,879) at the different parking areas that are next to the border of the national park.

Whilst in the Berchtesgaden case the park has only a small number of entrances which are clearly defined, the situation in Mueritz National Park is much more complex. Because of many more access routes and great shares of visitors who come by bike, canoe, or simply hike into the reserve the method used in Berchtesgaden was not feasible for Mueritz.

Instead, two different methods of data creation were employed. One comprised intercept interviews (1,666) comparable to the Berchtesgaden study. The other was a random sampling of visitors at predefined census points throughout the national park. The object of the second was to obtain information on the number of visitors by activity types like cycling, canoeing or hiking. A subset of the passers-by was asked how long they stayed within the region, if they were overnight visitors and which accommodation type they had booked. This data was used for estimating the total number of visitors and for weighting the structured interviews. Because the 18 interview days were distributed according to seasonal, weekday and weather criteria, representative data could be obtained.

6.   Results

For Mueritz National Park about 390,000 visitors could be estimated in 2004, while there were approximately 1.13 million visitors in National Park Berchtesgaden in 2002. The visitors of both reserves were divided into two groups with reference to the national park as the decisive criterion to visit the region (Job et al. 2003). Using this procedure results in a proportion of 44% of national park tourists in a strict sense in the Mueritz region. The other 56% are designated as non-national park tourists. 77% of all interviewed visitors in the National Park Mueritz knew the status-category of the protected area correctly. Also the question about the role of the status as a national park can be assessed positively: For about 57% of the guests the status of a national park affected their decision to visit the region to a high or very high degree. Rather different are the findings in this context for the National Park Berchtesgaden: Just about 18% of the visitors answered that question in the same way described above. Nevertheless 57% of them knew the right category, although altogether just about 10% of all interviewed visitors could be designated as national park tourists in a strict sense. This severe discrepancy in the structure of the visitors can be explained by the different history of the national parks, but also because of the very long tradition of Berchtesgaden as an alpine tourism destination where the Park only plays a subordinate role.

All visitors of the National Park Mueritz generate an annual gross turnover of approximately 13.4 million euro. The value added rate for day trippers was about 37%, for the overnight tourists of about 40%. Thus a sum of income (direct and indirect) of 6.9 million euro can be estimated that is caused by tourism in the national park. About two-thirds of this sum account for the direct side and one-third for the indirect side of income. Taking into account only the national park tourists in a strict sense (generating an income of 2.9 million euro) and the average gross regional income per person in the Mueritz region (10,918 euro in 2004), the tourism originally induced by the national park creates 261 income equivalents. The results for the National Park Berchtesgaden are stated as follows: With a gross turnover of about 9.3 million euro and a total added value of 4.6 million euro as well as an average gross regional income per person of 22,500 euro (2002) 206 income equivalents are generated by the national park tourists in a strict sense. This less total effect – despite of the more than two-times higher attendance compared to the Mueritz National Park – reflects the fact of the rather low share of truly national park tourists in a clearer way.

National Park	Berchtesgaden	Mueritz
Visitors (sensu stricto)*	114,000	167,000
Visitors (in general)	1,129,000	390,000
Ø Daily expenditures per person*	57.50	43.90
Gross turnover*	12.1 million	7.3 million
Direct income*	4.05 million	2.6 million
Indirect income*	1.95 million	1.2 million
Sum of direct and indirect income*	6.0 million	3.8 million
Full Time Job Equivalent*	206 persons	261 persons

* national park tourists in a strict sense

Tab. 2: Economic effects (in US$) of national park tourism in two case study regions [3]

[3] Job et al. 2006

7. Discussion

Protected areas are increasingly seen as being economically and financially a great help to their surrounding communities (McNeely 1993). In addition to preserving biological values such set-aside areas have to contribute positively to economic welfare, otherwise acceptance, that is crucial for preservation is low, resulting in violation of protected areas' targets. Even though the intangible assets of protected areas are uncontested, those values are rather weak grounds for justifying protection over competing forms of land use, for those who have to bear the greatest costs. Tourism seems to help out in this context as it is one of the rare forms of use that is not excluded entirely from protected areas.

As the results stated above show, primarily two variables influence the regional economic impacts of tourism significantly: Firstly the total number of visitors and secondly the extent of their average daily expenditures during the stay. Especially the former should be estimated most accurately because deviations of this figure have a strong effect on the subsequent calculations. Furthermore the structure and the particular level of spending have to be surveyed separately for each region as it is not possible to generalise present findings at the moment. The surveys confirm previous studies in a way that tourists staying overnight – even when neglecting their expenditures on accommodation – cause a higher added value than day trippers.

For this reason overnight staying guests seem to be the more worthwhile target group, especially because of their different spatial behaviour that agrees in a better way with the concern of conservation of a protected area. This aspect implies two dimensions: First the absolute number of visitors could be diminished by a higher proportion of this segment as a result of their longer duration of stay (quantitative dimension). To achieve this, it could be expedient to upgrade the existing supply and thereby make new sources of income accessible (qualitative dimension). Packages in the tourism sector normally consist of many actors which have to collaborate positively to submit their offers. That is why close partnerships between all actors including the tourism, but also the conservation sector are necessary and e.g. successfully implemented within the region of National Park Mueritz (Job et al. 2004).

References

Archer, B.H. (1984): *Economic Impact: Misleading Multiplier.* Annals of Tourism Research 11/3: 517f..

Brandt, A/Klodt, T./Kramer, J./Ertel, R./Schasse, U./Revilla Diez, J. (2001): *Regionalwirtschaftliche Effekte der EXPO 2000 – Eine Schlussbilanz.* Hannover.

Breen, H./Bull, A./Walo, M. (2001): *A comparison of survey methods to estimate visitor expenditure at a local event.* Tourism Management 22/5: 473-479.

Del Valle, F.B.R. (2002): *The National Sanctuary Pampas del Heath: Case Study of a Typical "Paper Park" under Management of an NGO.* In: Terborg, J./van Schaik, C./Davenport, L./Rao, M. (eds.): Making Parks Work: Strategies For Preserving Tropical Nature (pp. 279-306). Washington, DC.

DOC (Department of Conservation) (2005): *General Policy for National Parks.* 01.08.2006. http://www.doc.govt.nz/About-DOC/Policies-Plans-and-Reports/General-Policy-Policy-for-National-Parks-2005/index.asp.

DTV (Deutscher Tourismusverband e.V.) (2005): *Natur .Erlebnis. Angebote. Entwicklung und Vermarktung, Leitfaden.* Bonn.

Dwyer, L./Forsyth, P./Spurr, R. (2004): *Evaluating tourism's economic effects: new and old approaches.* Tourism Management 25/3: 307-317.

Faulkner, B./Raybould, M. (1995): *Monitoring visitor expenditure associated with attendance at sporting events: An experimental assessment of the diary and recall methods.* Festival Management and Event Tourism 3/2: 73-81.

Fletcher, J. E. (1989): *Input-Output Analysis and Tourism Impact Studies.* Annals of Tourism Research 16/4: 514-529.

Hammer, T. (ed.) (2003): *Großschutzgebiete – Instrumente nachhaltiger Entwicklung.* Munich.

IUCN (The World Conservation Union) (2003): *Protected Areas Categories Task Force.* 25.01.2008. http://www.iucn.org/themes/wcpa/theme/categories/categories.htm.

IUCN (The World Conservation Union) (2005): *WCPA Strategic Plan 2005-2012.* Gland.

Job, H./Metzler, D./Vogt, L. (2003): *Inwertsetzung alpiner Nationalparks. Eine regionalwirtschaftliche Analyse des Tourismus im Alpenpark Berchtesgaden.* Kallmünz.

Job, H./Metzler, D./Müller, M./Mayer, M. (2004): *The Contribution of Small and Medium Tourism Enterprises to Regional Economic Development – a Comparison between two German National Park Regions.* In: Keller, P./Bieger, T. (eds.): The Future of Small and Medium Sized Enterprises in Tourism (= Editions AIEST Vol. 46, pp. 55-76). St. Gallen.

Job, H./Harrer, B./Metzler, D./Hajizadeh-Alamdary, D. (2005): *Ökonomische Effekte von Großschutzgebieten.* Untersuchung der Bedeutung von Großschutzgebieten für den Tourismus und die wirtschaftliche Entwicklung der Region (= BfN-Skripten 135). Bonn-Bad Godesberg.

Job, H./Metzler, D. (2006): *Naturparke + Tourismus = Regionalentwicklung?* Natur und Landschaft 81/7: 355-361.

Job, H./Metzler, D./Woltering, M. (2006): *Large scale Protected Areas + Tourism = Regional Development?* In: Siegrist, D./Livaz, C./Hunziker, M./Iten, S. (eds.): Proceedings of the Third International Conference on Monitoring and Management of Visitor Flows in Recreational and Protected Areas. "Exploring the Nature of Management" (pp. 140-144). Rapperswil.

Job, H. (2008): *Estimating the regional economic impact of tourism to national parks.* In: GAIA 17/S1: 134-142.

Küpfer, I. (2000): *Die regionalwirtschaftliche Bedeutung des Nationalparktourismus untersucht am Beispiel des Schweizerischen Nationalparks.* Zernez.

Leiper, N. (1999): *A conceptual analysis of tourism-supported employment which reduces the incidence of exaggerated, misleading statistics about jobs.* Tourism Management 20/5: 605-613.

McNeely, J. A. (eds.) (1993): *Parks for Life: Report of the IVth World Congress on National Parks and Protected Areas.* Gland.

Metzler, D. (2007): *Regionalwirtschaftliche Effekte von Freizeitgroßeinrichtungen – Eine methodische und inhaltliche Analyse.* Kallmünz.

Mules, T. (2004): *Value of Tourism.* In: An assessment of the values of Kosciuszko National Park (pp. 233-238). Fyshwick.

Patriquin, M.N./Alavalapati, J.R.R./Wellstead, A.M./White, W.A. (2002): *A comparison of impact measures from hybrid and synthetic techniques: A case study of the Foothill Model Forest.* The Annals of Regional Science 36: 265-278.

Pearce, D./Turner, K. (1990): *Economics of Natural Resources and the Natural Environment.* Baltimore.

Samuelson, P. (1954): *The Pure Theory of Public Expenditure.* Review of Economics and Statistics 36/4: 387-389.

Schmidt, J. (2006): *Regionalökonomische Wirkungen von Großschutzgebieten. Eine empirische Studie zu den Nationalparken in Deutschland.* Hamburg.

Strasdas, W. (2001): *Ökotourismus in der Praxis, Zur Umsetzung der sozio-ökonomischen und naturschutzpolitischen Ziele eines anspruchvollen Tourismuskonzeptes in Entwicklungsländern.* Ammerland.

Strasdas, W. (2004): *The Global Market of the Nature-based Tourism.* In: Job, H. and Li, J. (eds.): Natural Heritage, Ecotourism and Sustainable Development. Potentials and Pitfalls for China (pp. 55-64). Kallmünz.

Strasdas, W. (2004): *Tourismus und Naturschutz – Duell oder Duett?* Integra 2/2007: 2-6.

Thorbecke, E. (1985): *The Social Accounting Matrix and Consistency-Type Planning Models.* In: Pyatt, G./Round, J. (eds.): Social Accounting Matrices: A Basis for Planning (pp. 20-256). Washington, DC.

VDN (Verband Deutscher Naturparke e.V.) (2006): Press release: *Nationale Naturlandschaften liegen im Reisetrend.* Bonn.

Wagner, J.E. (1997): *Estimating the Economic Impacts of Tourism.* Annals of Tourism Research 24/3: 592-608.

Walpole, M.J./Goodwin, H.J./Ward, K.R.G.R. (2001): *Pricing Policy for Tourism in Protected Areas: Lessons from Komodo National Park, Indonesia.* Conservation Biology 15/1: 218-227.

WCPA (World Commission on Protected Areas) (1998): *Economic Values of Protected Areas: Guidelines for Protected Area Managers.* Gland.

Yuan, M./Yuan, S. (1996): *Sixteen versus Nine Expenditure Categories in Tourism Surveys: Is There a Difference?* Journal of Travel Research 34/4: 59-62.

Tourism in Protected Areas
- A New Zealand Perspective

Michael Lück

1. Introduction

Since the establishment of the world's first national park in 1872, Yellowstone National Park in Wyoming/USA, tourists and recreationists alike have sought the beauty of these protected areas. Naturally, humans have been attracted to the features of outstanding natural beauty in the parks, such as mountains, lakes, shores, forests, deserts, volcanoes, and the like. Depending on the location, size, features, and accessibility of the park, annual visitor numbers can vary significantly. For example, the Great Smokey Mountains National Park in Tennessee and North Carolina, USA, attracted over 9.3 million visitors in 2002, while in the same year Paparoa National Park in New Zealand was visited by a "mere" 43,500 nature lovers (Department of Conservation, 2008a; wiseGeek, 2008). Managing large visitor numbers in protected areas is a major challenge for the conservation agencies involved. Their mandate is twofold, with conservation on the one hand, and making visitor access possible on the other. In cases, such as New Zealand, the National Park Act states that the public must have *free* access to the conservation estate. In the United States, on the other hand, visitors are being charged entry fees at most national parks. Butler and Boyd (2000, 3) refer to this interaction between tourism/recreation and conservation as a "long but uneasy relationship."

This chapter looks at tourism in New Zealand, and its significance to the country's economy, before introducing New Zealand's protected areas, associated legislation, and its application to tourism in New Zealand.

2. Tourism in New Zealand

Shortly after the arrival of the first European settlers in the 1840s, New Zealand attracted its first tourists. The famous playwright and critic George Bernard Shaw visited New Zealand for four weeks in 1934. Having been beleaguered by journalists asking what he thought of New Zealand, he increasingly resorted to answers, such as "Altogether too many sheep", or, referring to the geothermal reserve in Rotorua, "this must be the gateway to hell." (Bain, 2006, 40; Hells Gate Waiora Spa, 2007). However, not every traveller to New Zealand thought poorly about the country, and growth in tourism started early. New Zealand established the world's first governmental department for the development of tourism; the New Zealand Department of Tourist and Health Resorts (Collier, 2006). As in many other countries, tourism development was also closely linked to the introduction and expansion of a railway network. As early as in the early 1900s, a number of towns and resorts, such as Rotorua, Hanmer Springs, and the Hermitage at Mount Cook were already served. It was recognised in the early days that national parks are not only of intrinsic, but also of commercial value. Thus, it was suggested that national parks should be established along the main railway trunk routes, in order to attract many visitors, and subsequently profits for the railway company (Booth & Simmons, 2006). Since 1922 tourist numbers to New Zealand have been officially recorded. In 1922, 8050 people visited New Zealand as tourists, and spent about £100 each (Collier, 2006). Tourism grew steadily (with the exception of the World War II years), and in 1991 the New Zealand Tourism Board (NZTB, the governmental body to promote New Zealand as a tourism destination overseas) predicted three million visitors for the year 2000. However, this target was too ambitious, and New Zealand hosted 1.9 million visitors in 2000. Since the 1990s there has also been a shift in the strategy of the NZTB: Instead of rapidly increasing tourist numbers, the NZTB launched a new campaign targeting the "interactive traveller". The focus was on the more sophisticated and affluent high quality traveller, rather than just on numbers. In the foreword of the New Zealand Tourism Forecasts 2006-2012 Summary Document (Ministry of Tourism - Te Manatū Tāpoi, 2006, 1), the Minister of Tourism notes that he is "very mindful that the forecasts are focussed on numbers, whereas what is ultimately important for us all is the yield we gain from these visitors." In the year ended November 2007, a total of 2.46 million overseas visitors entered New Zealand (Ministry of Tourism, 2008). The domestic market is an important economic factor as well. New Zealanders took more than 30.6 million day trips, and 15.2 million overnight stays, with a total of 44.9 million nights. These numbers are reflected in the significant contribution to the New Zealand economy. International expenditure (excluding international airfares) was $NZ 6.291 billion, and domestic expenditure was $NZ 7.896 billion ($NZ 2.838 billion day trip spend, and $NZ 5.058 overnight trip spend) (Ministry of Tourism, 2008). The combined spending thus tallied up at $NZ 18.6 billion (incl. international airfares), which represented an 8.9% contribution to New Zealand's total GDP (Ministry of Tourism, 2008).

New Zealand has long maintained a "clean green" image, and attracts nature based tourists to a large extent. The main attractions in the country are indeed based on the natural environment, such as geothermal areas and hot springs, fiords, lakes and rivers, coastlines and cliffs, alpine regions with mountains and glaciers, and various wildlife based activities. Almost every tourist coming to New Zealand becomes a nature based tourist at least during some parts of their stay. Table 1 shows the activities undertaken by tourists in the year ending March 2007. Clearly, activities such as eating out and shopping are part of every holiday. These "general" activities are closely followed by a number of nature-based activities, such as walks, beaches, boat cruises, gardens and parks, lookouts, and the like.

Table 1: Activities/Attractions in NZ[1]

Activities/Attractions	YE Mar 07
Eating Out/Restaurants	69%
Shopping	67%
Walk In City	57%
General Sightseeing	48%
Visit Friends/Family/People	45%
Beaches	38%
Geothermal Attractions	27%
Lookouts And Viewing Platforms	27%
Botanical Gardens/Private Gardens	26%

---

[1] The International Visitor Survey is a sample-based survey of departing international visitors aged 15+ years. The sample is weighted up to match the number of departing international visitors. Because the IVS is representative of international visitor flows and behaviour, numbers are smaller for less frequented places, activities, transport types and so forth (Ministry of Tourism, http://www.tourismresearch.govt.nz/).

Museums	26%
Scenic Boat Cruise	25%
Gondola/Cable Car/Tram Ride	20%
Scenic Drive	17%
Historic Buildings	17%
Lakes	17%
Bar/Nightclub	17%
Maori Performances	16%
Hot Pools	16%
Business	15%
Bush Walk 1/2 Day	13%
Sightseeing Tour (Land)	13%
Glow Worm Caves	13%
Historic Sites	12%
Non-specific Walk	12%
Zoos/Wildlife/Marine Parks	11%
Art Galleries	10%
Bush Walk 1/2 Hr	10%
Jet Boating	9%
Glacier Walk	9%
Trekking/Tramp (At Least 1 Day)	9%
Waterfalls	9%
Wine Trail/Vineyards	8%
Cinema/Movies	7%
Farm Show	7%
Seal Colony	6%
Scenic Flight (Heli, Plane)	6%
Family Event	6%
Marae Visits	6%
Penguins	6%
Dolphin Watching/Swimming	5%
Theme And Leisure Parks	5%
Major Art/Culture Event	5%
Milford Sound	5%
Glaciers	5%
Casinos	5%

Farm Tour	5%
Swimming	5%
Bungy Jumping	5%
Other Natural Attractions	5%
Whale Watching	5%

3. New Zealand's National Parks and Protected Areas

New Zealand's protected areas are subdivided in terrestrial protected areas and marine protected areas (MPAs). Today, about 31% of New Zealand's land is protected in one way or the other, with a third out of these (10%) being national parks. The Department of Conservation is in charge of administering and managing this large amount of land. In contrast, less than 1% of New Zealand's extensive marine environments are protected in form of marine protected areas (Higham & Lück, 2007). There are a number of proposals for new protected areas, both terrestrial and marine.

3.1 Land Protected Areas

Only 22 years after the establishment of Yellowstone National Park in the USA, New Zealand was one of the first nations in the world to proclaim a national park in 1887. New Zealand's oldest national park was created due to the wise foresight of the Maori chief Te Heu Heu Tukino of the Ngati Tuwharetoa tribe. Te Heu Heu was aware that there would be claims of other Maori tribes and of European settlers for the three volcanoes on the central North Island (Mt. Ruapehu, Mt. Tongariro, Mt. Ngauruhoe), and thus this culturally significant area could subsequently be subdivided or lost to his tribe altogether. Although the details are not entirely clear, Booth and Simmons (2006) contend that the area around the three mountains was gifted by the Ngati Tuwharetoa to the New Zealand public with the condition of the formation of a public park. Today, New Zealand has a system of 14 national parks on the three main islands (North Island, South Island, Stewart Island). The youngest park is Rakiura National Park on Stewart Island (Table 2, Figure 1).

Table 2: New Zealand National Parks and Years of Establishment[2]

National park	Established
Tongariro National Park	1887
Egmont National Park	1900
Arthur's Pass National Park	1929
Abel Tasman National Park	1942
Fiordland National Park	1952
Aoraki/Mount Cook National Park	1953
Te Urewera National Park	1954
Nelson Lakes National Park	1956
Westland Tai Poutini National Park	1960
Mount Aspiring National Park	1964
Whanganui National Park	1986
Paparoa National Park	1987
Kahurangi National Park	1996
Rakiura National Park	2002

---

[2] Department of Conservation (http://www.doc.govt.nz/templates/NationalParks Landing.aspx?id=38405)

Figure 1: New Zealand National Parks[3]

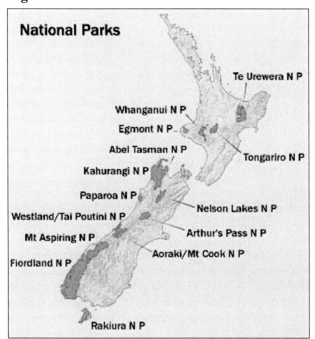

[3] Nature in New Zealand: The National Parks of New Zealand (http://www.nznature.co.nz/nznat/items/images/maps.jpg)

In addition to these 14 parks, there are currently eight new parks proposed:

- Auckland Volcanic Fields
- Waters and Seabeds of Fiordland
- Kahurangi NP, Farewell Spit, and Canaan Karst System
- Kerikeri Basin Historic Precinct
- Kermadec Islands
- Napier Art Deco Historic Precinct
- Whakarua Moutere (North East Islands)
- Waitangi Treaty Grounds Historic Precinct

In addition to the national parks, New Zealand has three designated World Heritage Areas: The Subantarctic Islands, Te Wāhipounamu - South West New Zealand World Heritage Area, and Tongaririo National Park.

In New Zealand, there is one governmental body who is in charge of the conservation estate; the Department of Conservation (DoC). DoC has its headquarter in the nation's capital, Wellington. It is subdivided into 14 conservancies, from north to south: Northland, Auckland, Waikato, Bay of Plenty, Tongariro/Taupo, East Coast/Hawkes Bay, Wanganui, Wellington, Chatham Islands, Nelson/Marlborough, West Coast, Canterbury, Otago, and Southland (Department of Conservation, 2007). Despite the recognition for the need to protect the natural environment, there are increasing voices that question whether it is necessary to have such large areas set aside for conservation purposes (see Box 1).

Box 1: Not everybody in New Zealand is in favour of the large areas set aside for conservation[4,5]

> ## Does DoC have too much land?
>
> DOES DOC have too much land? The National Party and high country farmers are calling for a debate on the issue now the department is responsible for 42 percent of the South Island and 17 percent of the North Island. DoC is in control of 31 percent of the whole country - up one percent since 2003.
>
> There needs to be a fresh look at DoC's priorities, says National conservation spokesman Nick Smith. "The ongoing expansion of the conservation estate is not necessarily the best way to protect native birds and species." But Forest and Bird says a lot of the DoC land was inherited because it is not suitable for farming.

3.2   Marine Protected Areas

New Zealand's remote geographical location, along with a number of islands belonging to the country, resulted in the country having one of the largest Exclusive Economic Zones (EEZs) in the world. In fact, the EEZ is 15 times larger than the land mass, and makes New Zealand the fourth largest maritime country in the world, covering 1.3 million square nautical miles (Figure 2).

---

[4] Inside Tourism. (2007, November 16). Does DoC have too much land? *Inside Tourism,* p. 1.

[5] Note: The National Party is currently in the opposition.

Figure 2: The New Zealand Exclusive Economic Zone and Marine Protected Areas[6]

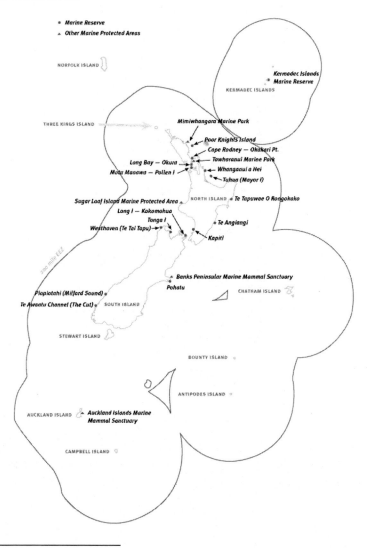

[6] From http://www.biodiversity.govt.nz/picture/doing/nzbs/part-three/theme-three.html

In contrast to the 30% of protected land, only about 3% of New Zealand's territorial sea (or 1% of New Zealand's EEZ) are protected. Furthermore, 99% of these protected waters lie in two extremely remote off-shore island groups, the Kermadec Islands (some 1000 kilometers to the north-east of New Zealand), and the Auckland Islands (about 460 kilometers south of the South Island), which leaves only small areas protected around the three main islands (North Island, South Island, Stewart Island). However, according to the Department of Conservation (2008b) the "New Zealand Biodiversity Strategy (2000) goal includes having 10% of the marine environment in a network of Marine Protected Areas by 2010". This goal was reemphasised by New Zealand's Minister of Tourism, the Hon. Damien O'Connor, in his opening address at the 5th International Coastal & Marine Tourism Congress in Auckland, in September 2007.

There are currently 22 marine reserves, four marine parks, and a number of other MPAs, such as Mataitai (areas of traditional importance to Maori for food gathering), Taipure (areas where special value to iwi or hapu is recognised), wildlife sanctuaries and refuges, marine mammal sanctuaries, and areas of significant conservation value (Fig. 2) (Department of Conservation, 2008b).

4. New Zealand's Protected Areas and Tourism, and Regulation

In New Zealand, it is difficult to differentiate between nature-based tourists and "general" tourists. In fact, the majority of visitors to New Zealand have been attracted by New Zealand's image as a country of outstanding natural beauty. Even the typical mass tourist travels through the most stunning countryside, visits national parks, or takes a cruise on Milford Sound. Thus, apart from conference/convention travel and business travel, it would be fair to assume that the majority of international tourists are indeed nature-based tourists. According to the Department of Conservation (2008a), 704,600 international tourists (32.25%) visit at least one national park during their stay. The most visited national parks, Fiordland and Westland, counted 431,000 and 405,500 visitors in 2006, respectively. Kearsley (1997) recognised a significant increase in the so-called "soft", "eco" or "green" tourism since the late 1980s. Higham and Carr (2003) note that the tourism environment in New Zealand has been changing due to a number of external factors, such as the September 11 attacks in 2001, and the Asian Economic Crisis in 1997-1998. Despite these fluctuations in the tourism generating markets, they agree with Kearsley and contend that "[o]ne constant in the otherwise changeable New Zealand tourism industry has been the importance of nature-based visitor experiences, and the growth of the ecotourism sector" (2003, 19). While the rise in nature-based and ecotourism demand is laudable, and it can bring in significant revenue, Kearsley (1997) warns that the pressures on the natural environment have grown more than the overall visitor numbers. He argues that this is the result of the increase in nature-based tourism, and the shift from pre-arranged packed tourism to FIT tourism.

The overarching piece of legislation for planning and managing New Zealand's resources is the Resource Management Act 1991 (RMA). After years of consultation, the RMA brought together a number of older pieces of legislation under a single statutory regime for the management of natural and physical resources (Hall, *in press*). The core of the RMA is the promotion of the sustainable management of New Zealand's resources, as outlined in Part 2, Section 5, Paragraph 2 of the RMA (in Hall, *in press*):

(2) In this Act, sustainable management means managing the use, development, and protection of natural and physical resources in a way, or at a rate, which enables people and communities to provide for their social, economic, and cultural wellbeing and for their health and safety while –
   (a) Sustaining the potential of natural and physical resources (excluding minerals) to meet the reasonably foreseeable needs of future generations; and
   (b) Safeguarding the life-supporting capacity of air, water, soil and ecosystems; and
   (c) Avoiding, remedying, or mitigating any adverse effects of activities on the environment.

It is important to note that the RMA explicitly mentions the coastal and marine area as one of the important matters. It is also noteworthy that the RMA is not legislation specifically implemented for tourism development and management, but that it applies to tourism and recreation developments.

In order to manage terrestrial parks appropriately, the Department of Conservation developed management plans for each national park. These plans include an extensive inventory of the assets of the park, including natural and human values. The latter is comprised of heritage and cultural values, user values, such as the various (recreational/touristic) activities, and of commercial values (e.g., grazing, hunting and trapping, and filming as a specialised commercial use) (Department of Conservation, 1994). Management plans, such as the Mount Aspiring National Park Management Plan, then go on and analyse the threats and opportunities to the parks and their values. In particular, tourism development represents the majority of threats, but also the majority of opportunities. Among the main threats are noise pollution, for example, from traffic, jet boats, air traffic (both helicopters and fixed wing), visual intrusion, the erection and maintenance of facilities (such as huts, rest areas, toilet facilities), and crowding. Non-tourism related threats include fire risks and the extraction of minerals and other resources. On the other hand, the Mount Aspiring National Park Management Plan identifies a long list of opportunities, which are almost directly or indirectly connected with tourism and recreation. These include not only the common tourist use, but also filming, education, and research opportunities (Department of Conservation, 1994). The second half on the document then introduces the policies related to the park. The Mount Aspiring National Park Management Plan (1994, 39) identifies four primary objectives:

- **Primary Objective 1**
  To preserve in perpetuity the landscape, ecological systems, natural and historic features of Mount Aspiring National Park and as far as possible eradicate introduced plants and animals.
- **Primary Objective 2**
  To retain the essential character of Mount Aspiring National Park as a remote, undeveloped, natural area of great beauty and of value for recreation, appreciation and study.
- **Primary Objective 3**
  To give the public the opportunity to gain benefit, enjoyment, inspiration and opportunities for recreation from the park to the extent compatible with primary objectives 1 and 2.
- **Primary Objective 4**
  To have regard to the Principles of the Treaty of Waitangi as defined by the Court of Appeal (1987).

These objectives reflect the National Park Act (1980), and try to balance the core principles of access for the public on one hand, and the need for conservation on the other.

Due to the lack of physical borders, the marine environment is regulated by a mix of international regulations (e.g., the International Convention for the Prevention of Pollution from Ships [MARPOL], and the International Convention on the Control of Harmful Anti-fouling systems on ships [Anti-fouling Convention]) and national legislation (e.g., the RMA, including the New Zealand Coastal Policy Statement [NZCPS]). Due to the enormous growth of whale and dolphin watching in New Zealand since 1989, the Marine Mammal Protection Act (1978) and the Marine Mammal Protection Regulations (1992) are of particular interest to tourism in coastal and marine environments. The MMPA and MMPR have been developed in order to protect marine wildlife. Constantine (1999, 8) states the purpose of these two regulations:

To make provision for the protection, conservation, and management of marine mammals and, in particular:
  (a) To regulate human contact or behaviour with marine mammals either by commercial operators or other persons, in order to prevent adverse effects on the interference with marine mammals;
  (b) To prescribe appropriate behaviour by commercial operators and or other persons seeking to come into contact with marine mammals.

Since there have not been any commercial whale watching activities in New Zealand when the MMPA came into effect in 1978, and the whale watching industry (including dolphin watching) grew rapidly in the early 1990s, a set of rules pertaining to these activities were implemented as early as in 1992 – the MMPR. According to Part I of the regulations, no commercial operation is to be carried out without a valid permit. Currently, there are more than 75 permits for commercial whale and dolphin watch operations issued (Brown, 2000). The MMPR also regulate the behaviour of licensed operators and private boaters around marine mammals. For example, for interactions with dolphins, regulations require boast to approach a pod at no-wake speed and only from behind or the sides, so as to minimise the agitation of dolphin groups. In order to limit noise, disturbance and stress of dolphins, there are only three vessels allowed within 100 meters of a dolphin or a pod at any one time. Vessel operators are not allowed to obstruct the path of any dolphin (Markowitz, Harlin, & Würsig, 1999). Figures 3-5 illustrate the regulations for behaviour around whales and dolphins, and regulations for operators of aerial whale and dolphin watching activities.

Figure 3: Regulations governing vessel operations around whales[7]

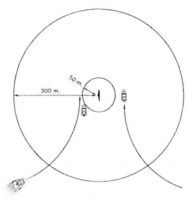

- Minimum approach distance of 50 metres
- 'No wake' speed within 300 m.
- Approach from behind and parallel to Whale(s).
- No more than 3 vessels within 300 m.
- Path of Whale(s) not to be obstructed.

Figure 4: Regulations governing vessel operations around dolphins[7]

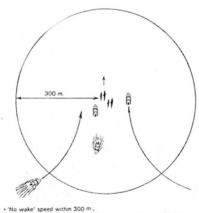

- 'No wake' speed within 300 m.,
  On departure greater speeds can be used to outdistance dolphins.
- Approach from behind and parallel to Dolphins.
- No more than 3 vessels within 300 m.
- Path of Dolphins not to be obstructed.

---

[7] Marine Mammal Protection Regulations (1992)

Figure 5: Aircraft approach distances to marine mammals[7]

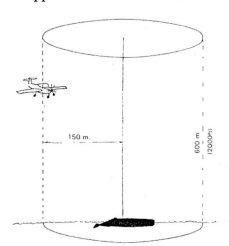

150 m.

600 m. (2000ft)

In addition, Part III also requires a variety of tour operator behaviour, such as no rubbish to be thrown over board near a marine mammal, swimming with juvenile dolphins is prohibited, interaction is to be abandoned if there is any sign of the mammal being disturbed or alarmed, and many more. Markowitz et al. (1999, 2) refer to Hardin (1968) and state that "by restricting the access of capitalist enterprises to this natural resources, the New Zealand Department of Conservation has effectively avoided the "Tragedy of the Commons".' They suggest that the DoC model in New Zealand could be a role model for the management of marine mammal tourism at other locations around the globe.

5. Conclusions

New Zealand has some outstanding natural resources of highest international standard. The country has been able to promote itself as a clean and green destination for nature loving international tourists. In particular, New Zealand's protected areas, both terrestrial and coastal/marine, have been at the top of the "must see" lists of many tourists. While about one third of New Zealand's land is protected in some form, the protection of its marine environment lacks behind with currently just about 3%. However, the current Labour government made a commitment to have at least 10% of the marine environment protected by 2010. Tourism puts the natural environment in New Zealand under considerable stress, especially at bottle-neck locations, and/or locations of high interest to tourists – mostly those with unique natural features, such as the fiords in Southland/Fiordland, and the geysers around Rotorua and Taupo. The Crown's agency for the management of New Zealand's conservation estate, the Department of Conservation, has management plans in place, and manages the land and waters in accordance with a variety of legislative regulations, such as the Resources Management Act 1991, and the Marine Mammals Protection Act 1992. It is vital for the health of New Zealand's natural environment to sustainably exploit these resources, so that DoC's two main mandates – access for the public and conservation – can be achieved. The increasing significance of tourism to New Zealand's economy (in recent years tourism overtook agriculture and is now the country's number one foreign exchange earner) and the related possible negative impacts make it increasingly difficult to sustainably manage the conservation estate and the natural environment in general.

References

Bain, C. (2006). *New Zealand.* Oakland, CA: Lonely Planet.

Booth, K. L., & Simmons, D. G. (2006). Tourism and the establishment of national parks in New Zealand. In R. W. Butler & S. W. Boyd (Eds.), *Tourism and National Parks: Issues and Implications* (pp. 39-49). Chichester: John Wiley & Sons.

Brown, N. C. (2000). *The Dusky Dolphin, Lagenrhynchus obscurus, off Kaikoura, New Zealand: A Long-term Comparison of Behaviour and Habitat Use.* Unpublished MSc Thesis, University of Auckland, Auckland.

Butler, R. W., & Boyd, S. W. (2000). Tourism and parks - a long but uneasy relationship. In R. W. Butler & S. W. Boyd (Eds.), *Tourism and National Parks: Issues and Implications* (pp. 3-11). Chichester: John Wiley & Sons.

Collier, A. (2006). *Principles in Tourism - A New Zealand Perspective* (7th ed.). Auckland: Pearson Hospitality Press.

Constantine, R. (1999). *Effects of tourism on marine mammals in New Zealand* (Vol. 106, Science for Conservation Series). Wellington: Department of Conservation.

Department of Conservation. (1994). *Mount Aspiring National Park Management Plan.* Wellington: Department of Conservation (DoC).

Department of Conservation. (2007). *By Region.* Retrieved February 5, 2008

Department of Conservation. (2008a). *International visitor numbers to selected National Parks.* Retrieved February, 6, from http://www.doc.govt.nz/templates/openpage.aspx?id=44861

Department of Conservation. (2008b). *Marine reserves & other protected areas.* Retrieved February, 4, 2008, from http://www.doc.govt.nz/templates/summary.aspx?id=33756

Hall, C. M. (in press). Coastal Tourism Planning and Policy in New Zealand. In R. K. Dowling & C. Pforr (Eds.), *Coastal Tourism Development: Planning and Management Issues.* Elmsford, NY: Cognizant Communications.

Hardin, G. (1968). The Tragedy of the Commons: The population problem has no technical solution; it requires a fundamental extension in morality. *Science, 162* (December), 1243 - 1248.

Hells Gate Waiora Spa (2007). *George Bernard Shaw.* Retrieved February 7, 2007, from http://www.hellsgate.co.nz/Hells_Gate/George_Bernard_Shaw_IDL=2_IDT =627_ID=3505_.html

Higham, J., & Carr, A. (2003). Defining Ecotourism in New Zealand: Differentiating Between the Defining Parameters with a National/Regional Context. *Journal of Ecotourism, 2*(1), 17-32.

Higham, J., & Lück, M. (2007). Marine Wildlife and Tourism Management: In Search of Scientific Approaches to Sustainability. In J. Higham & M. Lück (Eds.), *Marine Wildlife and Tourism Management: Insights from the Natural and Social Sciences* (pp. 1-16). Wallingford: CAB International.

Kearsley, G. W. (1997). Managing the Consequences of Over-use by Tourists of New Zealand's Conservation Estate. In C. M. Hall, J. Jenkins & G. Kearsley (Eds.), *Tourism Planning and Policy in Australia and New Zealand: Cases, Issues and Practice* (pp. 87-98). Sydney: Irwin.

Markowitz, T., Harlin, A., & Würsig, B. (1999). *New Zealand Dusky Dolphins* (Earthwatch Field Report). Laredo, Texas and Kaikoura, New Zealand: Earthwatch & Department of Wildlife and Fisheries Science, Texas A&M University.

Ministry of Tourism - Te Manatū Tāpoi. (2006). *New Zealand Tourism Forecasts 2006-2012 Summary Document.* Wellington: Ministry of Tourism - Te Manatū Tāpoi.

Ministry of Tourism. (2008). *Key Tourism Statistics.* Wellington: Ministry of Tourism.

wiseGeek. (2008). *Which U.S. National Parks Have the Most Visitors?* Retrieved February, 6, from
http://www.wisegeek.com/which-us-national-parks-have-the-most-visitors.htm

Towards sustainable stewardship:
The case of Gunung Rinjani National Park

Fleur Fallon

Lombock Peak [Gunung Rinjani] ... is the culminating point, formed a fit background to a view scarcely to be surpassed either in human interest or picturesque beauty.

Alfred Russel Wallace 1989, 174 (1869), *The Malay Archipelago*

1. Introduction

In 2004, the World Legacy Destination Stewardship Award was presented by Queen Noor of Jordan to Gunung Rinjani National Park (GRNP), Lombok island, Indonesia and the Rinjani Trek Management Board (RTMB). This was one of several awards related to efforts in sustainable tourism and sponsored by the National Geographic Society and Conservation International. This award recognises the significant efforts made over a five year period by the stakeholders of Rinjani and supported by NZAid (New Zealand Agency for International Development) funding. However, given the location of the Park which intersects three local government jurisdictions and multiple agencies involved in aspects of Rinjani care and protection, resolving disputes between various stakeholders is an ongoing task, regardless of whether tourists visit the mountain or not. The park, business and community partnership is a delicate balancing act.

This paper introduces the background of Rinjani and Lombok within the context of ecologically sustainable tourism, that is tourism that implies an 'ongoing concern for the maintenance of those environmental qualities which attract and give satisfaction to visitors...'(Pigram 1995, 208, cited in Fallon 2002, 166). Additionally, there is a central consideration in relation to sustainability, as defined by the WCED Report (World Commission on Environment and Development 1987). For whom is the activity sustainable? What claims of justice and equity are made, not only for future generations, but for the community located within and close by the National Park? What links are there between the economic activity and the local community, often ignored and marginalised in the decision-making processes? The discussion highlights the challenges involved in sustainable stewardship and makes some recommendations.

2. Background

2.1 Geography

Lombok, meaning 'chilli pepper', is one of more than 17,000 islands in Indonesia, and one of two main islands that comprise the province of West Nusa Tenggara (Nusa Tenggara Barat, hereafter NTB). The other main island is Sumbawa, to the east, separated from Lombok by the Alas Strait. Lombok is located east of Bali between 8 and 9 degrees south of the equator, and between 115 to 117 degrees longitude (see Figure 1).

At its widest points, Lombok is approximately 80 kilometres west to east and 70 kilometres north to south. It is traversed by a volcanic mountain range, dominated by the imposing Gunung Rinjani, 3,726 metres high, the highest mountain outside West Papua (formerly known as Irian Jaya) in the Indonesian archipelago. In 1901 an eruption created a new volcanic cone, Gunung Baru, in Rinjani's crater lake, Segara Anak. A smaller range of volcanic hills and mountains lies to the south of the island.

The central plain is very fertile, and well-watered, permitting a wide range of crops to be grown. Lombok has two seasons: a dry season from April to September and a wet season from October to March. The temperature ranges from 21–33 degrees centigrade, with high levels of humidity. Annual rainfall averages from 800–1000 millimetres (Resettlement and Infrastructure Agency NTB 2001), but there are immense spatial differences, ranging from about 700 millimetres in the driest part of Lombok on the east coast to over 3,500 millimetres in the Rinjani area (WSTCF 1993, in Monk, de Fretes & Reksodiharjo-Lilley 1997, 74). Parts of Lombok, particularly the south and south-east, are prone to long periods of drought, crop failure and famine.

Described by Alfred Wallace in 1869 as a prosperous island, blessed by nature, Lombok changed in less than one hundred years to an island with high levels of poverty (Van der Kraan 1976; 1980a; 1980b). This was the result of successive subjugation and exploitation by Balinese, Dutch, Japanese and Javanese rulers, as well as rapid population growth.

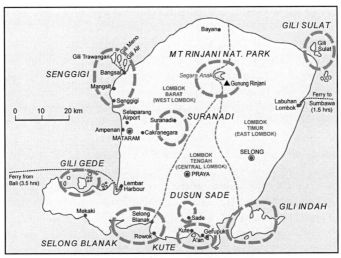

Figure 1: Lombok Regencies and Tourism Zones.
Adapted from NTB Provincial Tourism Office map.

2.2 The people

Lombok has a population of some 2.9 million, with an uneven distribution, ranging from less than 30 people per square kilometre in the north and south, to over 500 people per square kilometre in the central plains. In the provincial capital of Mataram, located in West Lombok, population density is 5,000 per square kilometre (NTB 1998; BAPPEDA NTB & Bogor Farming Institute 2000). Tirtosudarmo (1996, 199) surmises that, in Indonesia, 'Lombok is perhaps the only place that replicates Java's human ecological pattern,' that is, there is a very high population density. By comparison, Sumbawa, the other main island of NTB, is drier than Lombok, is three times larger, but has a population of only 1.5 million people. The population density on that island is only 69 people per square kilometre (KMNK 1999; NTB 1998).

The local community on Lombok is not necessarily a united, homogenous, and harmonious unit (Koeswadji 1975; Judd 1980; Gerdin 1982; Cederroth 1996). The indigenous people of Lombok, the Sasaks, comprise about 90 percent of the population. Throughout Indonesia, people were required to adopt one of four world religions: Islam, Buddhism, Hinduism or Christianity. Most people on Lombok are officially Muslim, but some, especially those in the north and north-west, still practise an indigenous syncretic faith that combines aspects of Hinduism, animism and Islam. Their religion is known as *wetu telu* (result of three), as distinct from *waktu lima* (five times) of orthodox Islam that requires prayer five times per day (see Cederroth 1996). The *wetu telu* group has experienced pressures to conform to orthodox Islam and discrimination as they do not belong to the 'true' Islam.

Additionally, the Sasaks are divided into a number of status groups, which vary between areas (Koeswadji 1975, 106–107). For example, the *wetu telu* Sasaks near Bayan, in the north of Lombok, are divided into three levels, with members of the middle level known by the title '*Lalu*'. In the central to south area of Lombok, the orthodox Muslim Sasaks have four levels; the highest uses the title of '*raden*', or '*lalu*' as per the Bayan Sasaks; the second level uses '*mamik*'; the third level is called '*bapa*'; and the lowest level is referred to as '*amak*'. Women in the first two levels are known as '*denda*' and '*baik*' respectively. Within these levels, different titles are used to differentiate further in terms of the 'purity' of their aristocratic descent (Koeswadji 1975, 107). Other members of Lombok's population include Balinese Hindu, mainly in West Lombok, as well as Arabs, Chinese, Javanese and people from the neighbouring islands of Sumbawa and Sulawesi. These groups include adherents of Christianity and Buddhism.

The development of tourism may further divide and highlight existing inequalities and differences within the community (Richards & Hall 2000). The different layers of government administration create additional complications in the management of local resources.

2.3 The government administration

The Governor of the province is appointed for a five year term. On Lombok there are four Regencies, or Districts on Lombok: *Kodya Mataram* (city of Mataram), *Lombok Barat (Lombar,* or West Lombok) with administrative offices in Mataram, *Lombok Tengah (Lomten,* or Central Lombok) with offices in Praya, and *Lombok Timur (Lomtim,* or East Lombok) with offices in Selong. Within these Regencies are sub-districts *(kecamatan),* villages *(desa)* and sub-villages or hamlets *(dusun).* For example, West Lombok has 9 sub-districts, 70 villages and 520 sub-villages; East Lombok has 10 sub-districts and 96 villages; Central Lombok has 9 sub-districts and 81 villages. Each village has an appointed village head *(kepala desa)* (NTB 1998). Gunung Rinjani National Park lies within the jurisdiction of the three districts outside of Mataram City.

3. Sustainable Tourism and the Environment

3.1 Tourism to NTB

Some indicators for tourism to NTB and in particular to GRNP are required prior to a discussion on sustainability. Due to the difficulty of obtaining accurate data, statistics should be seen as a guide to trends only (see Fallon 2002). Statistics provided by the Provincial Office of Culture and Tourism show an upward trend of foreign visitors to NTB until 1997, when they declined, but are again increasing, although domestic travellers have surpassed foreigners since 2000 (See Figure 2).

There are many factors that have negatively impacted on the tourism attractiveness of NTB and Indonesia as a whole since 1997. These include the economic crisis *(krismon)* of 1997, the political unrest leading up to President Soeharto's downfall in 1998, ethnic and religious conflicts, East Timor's bloody fight for independence and withdrawal of Indonesian troops in 1999, media reports of robbery and assault, riots on Lombok 2000, security threats following 9-11 with a spotlight on terrorists associated with Islam (the primary religion in Indonesia), the US-Iraq war, bombings in Bali 2002 and 2005, health threats from SARS and avian flu and foreign affairs travel advisories to stay away from Indonesia.

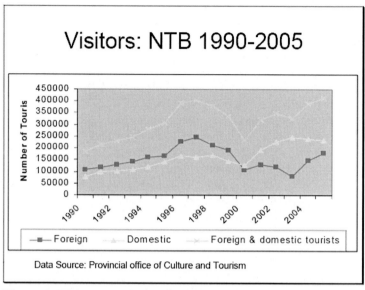

Figure 2: Visitors to NTB 1990-2005

Visitors to GRNP show a significant upward trend for domestic tourists and local visitors since the commencement of the GRNP Project (GRNPP) in 1999, while foreign visitors have remained relatively static, due to the level of fitness required to do the full trek to the top as well as the seasonal difficulties making an ascent virtually impossible in the rainy season (See Figure 3). With limited tourism activity, it may seem that discussion of sustainability is meaningless. However, it is emphasized that tourism is but one economic activity competing with others, and the protection of the area is not only necessary to ensure that it retains attractiveness for tourists, both domestic and foreign, but also retains economic and symbolic long-term enduring significance for the 80 communities that are located within or by the Park area.

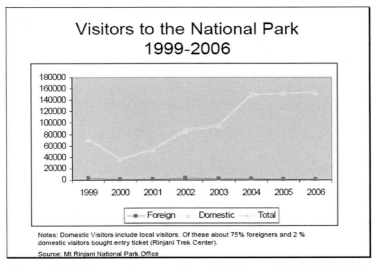

Figure 3: Visitors to Gunung Rinjani National Park 1999-2006

3.2 Competition for resources

The environment may exist without tourism, but some forms of tourism may lead to environmental destruction, thereby undermining the resource base it depends on for its healthy continuance. In addition, competition for scarce forest-, mountain-, water- and coastal resources has significant impacts on the local host communities. Some of these issues become increasingly complex and difficult to resolve against the background of a bewildering range of environmental laws and the laws pertaining to land ownership.

Information on Lombok's environmental factors has been fragmented and located in many offices, such as those responsible for domestic water supply, fisheries, coastal management, forestry and tourism. Bringing the information together emphasises the need for tourism to be integrated with other industry sectors for sustainable development considerations (Wall 1998). Similar issues arise for the planning and management of tourism as, for example, in forestry management. Both tourism and forestry management are closely linked in terms of sustainability issues. Both have a vested interest in the protection of the environment for

127

long-term use, yet both are likely to disturb and displace local communities who have traditionally derived their livelihoods by exploiting resources located in designated tourism and protected forest areas. The examination of these issues highlights the need for education, for community collaboration and assistance to local people to find alternative, or complementary, livelihoods, when aspects of the environment are designated as 'protected' and / or 'for tourism' (Son, Pigram & Rugendyke 1999).

3.3 Pressures on the environment

Even though economic growth has increased standards of health and education, the pressures of land use have created significant negative effects, especially in terms of the environment. Southeast Asia has suffered 49 percent forest loss due to timber exploitation in the latter part of the twentieth century. Before Rinjani was designated as a National Park, the Environmental Study Centre at Mataram University recorded 68 landslips around the Rinjani National Park area from 1985 to 1993 as a result of forest-cutting activities (WSTCF 1993, in Monk, de Fretes & Reksodiharjo-Lilley 1997, 65).

Whilst tourism, in particular nature tourism, depends on the environment for its continued attractiveness and desirability, it also has been a significant factor in development, because tourism requires access to, and control of, land that has long been in the hands of local communities. The effect of development on indigenous peoples is an illustration of the strong links between environmental protection and human rights. The weakest groups typically suffer the most from environmental degradation through the loss of their lands and, subsequently, often of their livelihood as well (Iorns & Hollick 1998, 7). Previously, those who dared to protest in Indonesia have been regarded as subversive and have been accused of acting against the national interest. Some groups may not have protested, either because they were not aware of the long-term implications, or because they had little formal knowledge of government processes and regulations. It may also be that some groups were simply afraid of the consequences of speaking out.

3.4 The State and the environment in Indonesia

Fisher, Moeliono and Wodicka (1998, 21) acknowledge that the 'dizzying array of rules, procedures and jurisdictions regarding the management of forest and conservation areas' that involve overlapping interests of different government groups present 'enormous challenges to co-ordination and effective decision making'. For a detailed discussion of legislation relating to the environment, see Fallon (2002).

Forest management

Fisher, Moeliono and Wodicka (1998) describe the challenges of forest and conservation management experienced on the fringes of the Gunung Rinjani National Park by the Nusa Tenggara Uplands Development Consortium, consisting of government agencies, NGOs, research institutions and local communities. The village of Rempek, to the north of Rinjani, has been the scene of forest boundary and land disputes, jurisdiction conflicts, encroachments, influx of migrants and logging. The disputes arose due to the contradictory policies of different government agencies. Added to this, conflicts with new migrants increased tensions in the community, which have led to public demonstrations, violence, encroachments on forest zones and repeated acts of sabotage of forestry projects.

In 1983, Sesaot, 20 kilometres from Mataram, and to the south-west of Rinjani, had its status changed from restricted production forest to protection forest (Fisher, Moeliono & Wodicka 1998, 10). The changed forest status aimed to protect the upper watershed for irrigation purposes, but has meant a decrease in income and made access difficult for the local population of approximately 11,000 residents. Many of these people came to the area for work in logging. Planting of mahogany as a main forest species has led to an inability to produce other crops due to the thick over storey cover; a 50 percent tax imposed on coffee production in the 'buffer zone was imposed as a disincentive to production', and the villagers were forbidden to gather forest products such as fuel-wood, animal fodder and timber. Increased landlessness, growing population pressure, exorbitant coffee taxes and illegal wood collection have combined to increase levels of conflict within the community and between the community and the government representatives.

Many of these problems arose due to conflicting policies of government departments and due to limited involvement in environmental decision-making by local communities. The agencies working in this program acknowledged the need for a broad-based systems perspective and analysis that involves a multi-community- inter-agency- ecosystems-based approach that engages and empowers local communities in a move towards 'more inclusive and sustainable approaches to management of protected areas' (Fisher, Moeliono & Wodicka 1998, 31). However, these moves towards collaborative all-inclusive approaches must be considered within the larger economic and political realities. Such collaborative processes are inevitably time-consuming, and may take community members away from income-producing activities. They are also constrained by hierarchical organisational structures that are characterised by inflexible policies and 'command-and-rule' cultures, limited budgets and frequent changes of public officials. These structures therefore may lack continuity and inhibit the process of developing a stronger institutional base (Fisher, Moeliono & Wodicka 1998, 37). However, they cannot be ignored and attempts at Participatory Action Research (PAR) have been made, involving 18 government agencies, 33 non-governmental agencies, one university and 33 representative villages from the 80 villages that are located in the Rinjani area (Astawa 2002). As well as issues of management on the boundaries of the National Park, there are considerable environmental management issues for the Park operators.

It is against the background of such dimensions of multiple conflicts for multiple stakeholders that the aim of sustainable tourism for GRNP is played out.

4. Gunung Rinjani National Park

The Rinjani area is significant for many reasons:

- For tourism
- Biodiversity of species
- As a major watershed for irrigation
- As a basis of economic life for local communities, who either clear the forest for agroforestry production such as coffee, candlenut, vanilla, fruit trees, or gather forest products, such as fuel-wood, timber for construction and animal fodder (Fisher, Moeliono & Wodicka 1998, 16).

Rinjani is Lombok's only National Park, established in May 1997. Previously it had been classified as a Wildlife Sanctuary. GRNP consists of 41,330 hectares and is surrounded by 66,000 hectares of Protection Forest, covering all three administrative districts on Lombok (GRNPP Newsletter No. 1, December 2000, 1). Rinjani is biologically diverse, with at least 33 mammal species and 136 bird species reported (Fisher, Moeliono & Wodicka 1998, 16). In addition to its biodiversity values, Rinjani is valued by both Balinese Hindus and Sasaks for spiritual reasons and for the healing powers of the hot springs near Segara Anak lake.

With increasing numbers making the Rinjani trek, locals as well as domestic and international tourists, the area has been degraded by human waste and other litter, erosion of tracks and deterioration of the limited facilities (GRNPP 2001). By July 2001, changes had taken place. Two metal composting toilets had been installed at Segara Anak lake and restrooms had been constructed at the two main Park gateways of Senaru and Sembalun Lawang. There are now regular clean-up campaigns. These initiatives were part of the Gunung Rinjani National Park project, a bilateral program between the governments of New Zealand and Indonesia. This initial three-year project (extended to mid-2008) commenced mid-1999 'to assist with the development of Gunung Rinjani National Park in a way that integrates the environmental and community development aims of the Indonesian Government' (Tourism Resource Consultants 2000, i).

The growing pressures on the Park by local communities and tourists, plus continuing political and social turbulence across Indonesia and assault and robbery on the mountain, all combined to exacerbate the urgent need for developing working partnerships between stake-holders. Furthermore, it was recognised that *adat*, the traditional custom of the people in the area, must be respected to ensure sustainable outcomes (Tourism Resource Consultants 2000, ii). The Park and therefore the Project is under the jurisdiction of the Directorate-General Nature and Conservation (PKA) within the Ministry of Agriculture and Forestry.

The Project recognises three key stake-holder groups: National Park managers, the communities on the Park boundaries and the tourism industry. Like the Nusa Tenggara Uplands Development Consortium working on the Park's boundaries, participatory management approaches designed to contribute to sustainable outcomes, both environmental and social, have been implemented.

There is a strong emphasis on human resource development and institutional strengthening. Indonesians are involved in key management positions with international consultants hired on a short-term basis only. Several training programs, for example, Search-and-Rescue, English language, guide training, national park and ecotourism awareness, First Aid, cooking and hygiene, village host training and small enterprise training have been conducted. The Project team has conducted surveys with the community to map and to assess the condition of the trek route and to analyse the quality of water supplies along the route. Trail maintenance has been completed and camp shelters have been repaired. The community mapping project has culminated in the production of a map and a brochure on 'What to do and see' in Senaru.

To reduce the risk of attacks on the mountain, all guides carry a two-way radio and, since January 2001, visitors to the mountain have been asked to sign a register. Trekkers to Rinjani in 2000 were mainly independent tourists, travelling as individuals, couples and small groups, who then arranged their treks after arrival on Lombok.

The Project has been working with the tourism industry in order to attract pre-booked groups of trekkers now that the security situation has improved. The Project also recognises that communities on the boundaries of the Park may create security issues if they are forced to cease livelihoods derived from the Park. GRNPP therefore 'will avoid advocating that poor farmers and other vulnerable stake-holders should make radical changes to their livelihood base on the assumption of growth in ecotourism' (GRNPP 2000, 1). Some detail about one of the key villages situated at the northern entrance to the National Park is presented here to emphasise some of the sensitive and difficult issues that need to be addressed in the quest to ensure that tourism programs in the area work towards the goal of genuine sustainability.

The village of Senaru is composed of 11 sub-villages and is located just west of Bayan (GRNPP Newsletter 2000, No.1, 3). There are nearly 7,000 inhabitants. Senaru administratively was part of Bayan until 1994 when it became a separate administrative area (community spokesperson, pers. comm. July 2001). The people are mostly farming small plots, growing coffee, coconut, cashew nuts, rice, onions, garlic and tobacco. The head of the village is from nearby Bayan village. Most of the administrative and key tourism positions in Senaru are held by the traditional aristocracy from Bayan or outsiders and not by Senaru local villagers. The small guest-houses are owned by people from Bayan, Mataram or Bali (GRNPP spokesperson, pers. comm. July 2001). Most of the Senaru villagers were not pro-active initially in setting up businesses for tourism, although active in developing informal businesses. The head of the village reported that the Participatory Rural Appraisal (PRA) process conducted by GRNPP helped the villagers to become familiar with the project. At first, there were some problems with adjusting to a new system of operations under the new Park management, such as working out the pricing system and rostering porters and guides.

The standard pricing for a three-night, two-day package in 2007 ranges from Rp2,036,000 for one person to Rp936,000 per person for a 11-20 person group[1]. A Park entry fee of Rp50,000 is also charged for foreigners[2]. Of this amount, Rp20,000 goes to the National Park, Rp7,500 goes to the Trek Office, Rp5,000 goes to Senaru village, and Rp12,500 for insurance for Search and Rescue purposes. Minimum daily rates for guides have been set at Rp75,000 and for porters at Rp60,000 (RTMB pers. comm. 2007). The entry fee for domestic visitors is Rp2,500, but many enter without paying a fee.

These set fees and the roster system have been accepted by the local villagers after a process of extensive consultation with the GRNPP members. By reducing competition and conflict between individuals and ensuring a fixed price and better quality standard equipment, it is apparent that a more equitable sharing of benefits has been achieved for the porters and guides who work in the Park. These are mostly male. Continuous consultation and negotiation is necessary to ensure a long term sense of fairness and equity is maintained. Further projects to involve women more in tourism in the Park have been initiated and include snack-making and some guided village tours (GRNPP spokesperson, pers. comm. July 2001; RTMB 2007b). The issues of gender as well as religious and traditional hierarchical 'patron-client' relationships have not been easy issues for the GRNPP to deal with and still need ongoing work.

---

[1] At November 2007, Rp13120 = Euro1.00. Park entry fee of Rp50,000 =Euro3.80
[2] This fee was increased to Rp150,000 for foreigners from 1 April 2008.

The results from the PRA process conducted in March–April 2000 indicated that the political reality of working at community level was going to be complex. While the national political situation meant that there was a greater acceptance of democratic and participatory management processes, there was a possibility that this could lead to increased cases of land encroachment and exploitation as old power structures could try to regain control of lost land and power. Political and religious pressures in the mid-1960s forced groups of villagers who had practised *wetu telu* Islam to conform to orthodox Islam. Now a critical younger generation is attempting to regain its identity. Outsiders, who have come to the area to work as sharecroppers or civil servants, hold greater bargaining power with government authorities as they practise 'true Islam'.

Women have been particularly disadvantaged and hold very few positions of importance. Issues for women include high illiteracy rates, high drop-out rates from school, early marriage and high divorce rates, and low self-confidence with few opportunities. The GRNPP identified élitism, leadership, gender, land access, language and education as key issues to be taken into consideration to identify target groups for increasing human resource skills and for developing genuine sustainability plans for tourism development in the area (GRNPP spokesperson, pers. comm. July 2001). For now, the market perceptions of security risks on Rinjani remain the biggest risk for the GRNPP. This has meant a decrease in the number of foreign visitors to the area and highlights 'the fact that ecotourism only works as a development tool if there is an on-going flow of tourists to the area' (GRNPP 2000, 20). GRNPP is working step-by-step to make positive changes on Rinjani for all stake-holders and to meet the demanding challenges of cross-sectoral co-ordinated decision-making that is a central process for sustainable development aims. The process must be ongoing and depends on persistent efforts by stakeholders, including continuity of positions held by those significant stakeholders.

The Vision of the RTMB is to build credible multi-stakeholder partnership in the management of eco-tourism in GRNP, with a focus on accountability, transparency, effectiveness and efficiency. The continuing link phase with New Zealand Aid extended from September 2006 to June 2008 encompasses a three circle approach with conservation of the Park, tourism and community development to reduce poverty and improve resource management extended to villages in the Park buffer zone.

The specific goals are to enhance the quality of products and services, through improving the skills and knowledge of guides and porters and to broaden RTMB's scope to assist other communities, for example, Timbanum to develop co-operative community programs for snack-making, cattle breeding, bamboo craft and semi-organic farming (RTMB 2007b). The third key goal is continual improvement of core eco-tourism structures of the Rinjani Trek. This involves monitoring and evaluating visitor impact, improving visitor management and feedback mechanisms, improving visitor satisfaction, removing rubbish, ongoing training for guides and porters and developing partnerships with travel agencies and tour operators.

Indicators of sustainability relate to three key areas: the environment, local community and economic returns to the local community. Specific measurements can be taken relating to the number of incidents of conflict in relation to land-use; degradation of resources due to visitation levels, illegal logging, litter, forest burn; level and frequency of participation by local people in planning and decision-making; as well as incidents relating to security, for example, crime, vandalism or robbery (see Fallon 2002, Table 11.1, 310-312; also UNWTO and Ministry of Culture and Tourism Indonesia 2007). It is recommended that the Rinjani stakeholders continually work to develop very specific, measurable indicators and implement a coherent monitoring and evaluation program and make regular adjustments as necessary.

5. Conclusion

The Rinjani Project has made considerable progress in seven years. Its ability to gather 'all the local players under one roof' and to develop a three-pronged approach for 'park management', 'community development' *and* 'tourism' is the corner-stone for its long term success (GRNPP 2003). It aims to establish good practices for developing partnerships for community-based tourism with the inclusion of the local community in decision-making and economic activity. Yet its continuation and partnership co-operation remains constantly vulnerable with uncertain funding futures, an unrealised tourism potential as well as ongoing conflicts and issues of representation in programs.

GRNP has been recognised as an iconic world destination by the Conservation International and *National Geographic* Destination Awards in

2004. With its emphasis on sound conservation principles, based on traditional knowledge, the Rinjani Ecotourism Programme was one of three 2008 finalists for the Tourism for Tomorrow Destination Award, announced by the World Travel and Tourism Council (WTTC) in Dubai, April 2008. The winner was Blackstone Valley, USA and the other finalist was from Canada. This is well deserved recognition of the determined work of all stakeholders to not only care for the destination to enhance its attraction for tourists, but also to develop micro-projects in adjoining villages in the buffer zone and place tourism as just one economic activity that must be integrated with others in the community.

Additionally, in 2007 a proposal was submitted to UNESCO's World Heritage Commission for inclusion of GRNP on the World Heritage Site listing. The outcome is pending (Jakarta Post 2007). Claims of success may well be validated if GRNP attains both the tourism award and World Heritage listing and through this may attract further external funding to support the continuation of the program. Success will not mean the end of journey, rather another step forward. The work must go on and the questions about 'for whom is the activity sustainable' and justice and equity must continue to be asked, to ensure that those who are most marginalized have improved chances at inclusion of such projects and can thus move closer towards that which we call 'sustainable development'.

A Rinjani ascent is not possible in the long wet season and only those with strong physical fitness and stamina can make it in the dry season. Gunung Rinjani is therefore unlikely to become a superhighway of tourism, and that too may well be a key saving grace in the context of sustainable stewardship.

Acknowledgements
Many thanks to Pak Asmuni and the team at the Rinjani Trek Managment Board (RTMB), previously known as the Gunung Rinjani National Park Project (GRNPP), Mal Clarbrough, Tourism Resource Consultants and Matthias Schellhorn, Lincoln University, for continuing open dialogue on the Rinjani Project.

References

Astawa, Budi (2002): Finding common ground in Rinjani, Lombok, Indonesia: Towards improved governance, conflict resolution, and institutional reform, dlc.dlib.indiana.edu/archive/00001526/00/Astawa_Finding_040802.pdf, (accessed 3 October 2007).

BAPPEDA NTB & Bogor Farming Institute (2000): Office of Coastal and Marine Resources: *Penyusunan rencana tata ruang wilayah pesisir dan laut pulau Lombok* (Draft plan for the zoning of coastal and marine resources for Lombok), Final report.

Barlow, Colin & Hardjono, Joan (eds) (1996), *Indonesia Assessment 1995: Development in Eastern Indonesia,* Institute of Southeast Asian Studies, Singapore & Research School of Pacific & Asian Studies, Canberra.

Cederroth Sven (1996): 'From ancestor worship to monotheism: Politics of religion in Lombok', *Temenos,* vol. 32:7–36, http://www.abo.fi/comprel/temenos/temeno32/cede.htm, (accessed 3 August 1999).

Fallon, Fleur (2002): Tourism Interrupted: The challenge of sustainability for Lombok Island, Indonesia 1987-2001. PhD thesis. University of New England, Australia.

Fisher, Larry, Moeliono, Ilya & Wodicka, Stefan, 1998, Alternative Approaches to Conflict Management. Cattle, cockatoos, chameleons, and ninja turtles - Seeking sustainability in forest management and conservation in Nusa Tenggara. 21 April, Indonesia International Development Research Centre (IDRC), http://www.idrc.ca/minga/case-in.html, (accessed 22 May 2001).

Gerdin, Ingela (1982): *The Unknown Balinese. Land, Labour and Inequality in Lombok,* Göthenburg Studies in Social Anthropology, Vol. 4, Göthenburg.

GRNPP (2003): Gunung Rinjani National Park Project, Good practices for community-based tourism in Rinjani National Park, Indonesia, Asia-Pacific Environmental Innovation Strategies (APEIS). Research on Innovative and Strategic Policy options (RISPO) http://www.iges.or.jp/APEIS/RISPO/inventory/db/pdf/0030.pdf, (accessed 3 October 2007).

GRNPP (2001): Gunung Rinjani National Park Project, *The Rinjani Trek Vision,* February, Mataram.

GRNPP (2000): Gunung Rinjani National Park Project Newsletter No. 1, December.

Iorns Magallanes, Catherine & Hollick, Malcolm (eds) (1998): *Land Conflicts in Southeast Asia,* White Lotus Press, Bangkok.

Jakarta Post (2007): Mount Rinjani up for world heritage list next year, 2 August, in UNESCO in the Indonesian News compilation of 2007, http://www.unesco.org.id/images/pub/91_listscience.doc (accessed 11 February 2008).

Judd, Mary (1980): The sociology of rural poverty in Lombok, Indonesia, PhD thesis, University of California-Berkeley.

KMNK (1999): (*Kantor Menteri Negara Kependudukan* – Ministry of Population) *Population of Indonesia 12 October*, Jakarta.

Koeswadji, Hermien (1975): 'The historical development of villages on the island of Lombok', *The Indonesian Quarterly*, vol. 3, no. 4:98–117.

Monk, Kathryn, de Fretes, Yance & Reksodiharjo-Lilley, Gayatri (1997): *The Ecology of Indonesia Series Volume V: The Ecology of Nusa Tenggara and Maluku*, Dalhousie University, Periplus Editions, Hong Kong.

NTB (1998): Nusa Tenggara Barat Provincial Government, *Welcome to Nusa Tenggara Barat*, Mataram.

Pearce, Douglas & Butler, Richard (eds) 1999, *Contemporary Issues in Tourism Development*, Routledge, London.

Pigram, John (1995): 'Resource constraints on tourism: Water resources and sustainability', in *Tourism Today: A Geographical Analysis* (ed) Douglas Pearce, Longman, London, pp.208–228.

Resettlement and Infrastructure Agency NTB (2001): Development program for settlement and infrastructure for NTB, Discussion paper, Mataram.

Richards, Greg & Hall, Derek (eds) (2000): *Tourism and Sustainable Community Development*, Routledge, London.

RTMB (2007a): Rinjani Trek Management Board, GRNP: Rinjani Trek Ecotourism Program Six months report continuing link phase.

RTMB (2007b): Rinjani Trek Management Board, Rinjani Trek Eco-tourism Report 2006-07, June.

Son, Nguyen Thi, Pigram, John & Rugendyke, Barbara (1999): 'Tourist development and National Parks in the developing world: Cat Ba Island National Park, Vietnam', in *Contemporary Issues in Tourism Development*, (eds) Douglas Pearce & Richard Butler, Routledge, London, pp.211–231.

Tirtosudarmo, Riwanto (1996): 'Human resources development in Eastern Indonesia', in *Indonesia Assessment 1995: Development in Eastern Indonesia*, (eds) Colin Barlow & Joan Hardjono, Institute of Southeast Asian Studies, Singapore & Research School of Pacific & Asian Studies, Canberra, pp. 198–212.

Tourism Resource Consultants (2000): Gunung Rinjani National Park Project. Inception Report, Vols. 1 & 2, NZODA-Indonesia Programme of the Ministry of Foreign Affairs and Trade, New Zealand, & the Government of the Republic of Indonesia, Mataram.

UNWTO and Ministry of Culture and Tourism Indonesia (2007): Summary report on Workshop on Indicators of Sustainable Development for Tourism Destinations: Lombok 21-24 March.

Van der Kraan, Alfons (1980a): *Lombok: Conquest, Colonization and Underdevelopment, 1870–1940*, Asian Studies Association of Australia Southeast Asia Publications Series No. 5, Heinemann Education Books, Singapore.

Van der Kraan, Alfons (1980b): *Dutch Rule in Lombok: The Development of Underdevelopment*, South East Asian Monograph Series, James Cook University, Townsville.

Van der Kraan, Alfons (1976): Selaparang under Balinese and Dutch colonial rule: A history of Lombok 1870–1940, PhD thesis, Australian National University, Canberra.

Wall, Geoffrey (1998): 'Reflections upon the state of Asian tourism', *Singapore Journal of Tropical Geography*, vol. 19, no. 2:232–237.

Wallace, Alfred Russel (1989) (1869): *The Malay Archipelago*, Oxford University Press, Oxford.

WCED (1987): World Commission on Environment and Development Report, *Our Common Future*, United Nations, New York.

WSTCF (1993): Water Sector Technical Co-operation Fund, Lombok water resources study. Final Report Volumes I and II, with CIDA, Jakarta.

Protected Areas in National Parks of Mexico
- Tourism as a Development Alternative

Oscar Mario Ibarra Martínez
Alexander Oliver Leibold Scherer

1. Background

1.1 Identification and terrain of Mexico

Mexico is a federal republic in the narrowest part of southern North America, bordering the United States in the north, the Gulf of Mexico and the Caribbean Sea in the east, Belize and Guatemala in the southeast and the Pacific Ocean in the west and south. The Mexican plateau dominates much of the country and is divided into two areas: northern and southern highlands, flanked by two mountain ranges which descend steeply to narrow coastal plains: the western and eastern Sierra Madre.[1]

Mexico is located in a transition zone between boreal and nearctic ecosystems, i.e. tropical and desert regions, which accounts for its diversity. The extensive coast and the mountainous terrain of Mexico primarily provide one of the largest varieties of ecosystems and habitats on Earth. The geographical position of the country has produced an eclectic mix of flora and fauna between the north and south. Mexico is just behind Indonesia, Brazil and Colombia in terms of its biodiversity.

Depending on its location and terrain, Mexico has varied climates conducive to the existence of a variety of ecosystems, such as areas with extreme temperatures, desert climate or high humidity:

- Warm and humid with rain in the summer or all year round.
- Warm humid climate and extremely low precipitation extremes with long periods of drought.
- Wet weather, extremely humid climate.
- Relatively warm and humid but in these areas frosts occur every year.

---

[1] "México (república)," Enciclopedia Microsoft® Encarta® Online 2007 http://mx.encarta.msn.com © 1997-2007 Microsoft Corporation.

- Dry. In these areas frosts occur every year.
- Very dry desert climate.

The Mexican Republic is extremely rich in almost all known minerals. Reserves of oil and natural gas are abundant, with some of the largest deposits in the world. In forests and forest lands, which cover 33.7% of the territory, trees of precious woods such as mahogany, sandalwood, ebony, red cedar, walnut, rosewood and Palo de Campeche grow. About 14.3% of the land is suitable for agriculture.

Thanks to the diverse climates, flora indigenous to Mexico is extremely varied. The prickly pear, yucca, guayule, the maguey (see Agave) and mesquite are abundant in the arid regions of the north. The area is covered by a huge variety of plants, which in some areas form dense rainforests. The trees in these areas include precious woods, coconut (see Palmáceas), chicozapote (from which chicle is obtained), tropical fruit trees such as mamey or guava, and kapok. Oak (see Encina), pine and Oyamel (see Abeto) grow on the hillsides. There is arctic vegetation in the higher elevations of Mexico.

Mexican wildlife also varies according to climatic zones. Wolves and coyotes live in the north; while the teporingo (volcano rabbit), a species endemic to Mexico, live in the higher areas of the Cordillera Neovolcanico. The forests of the mountain slopes are inhabited by ocelots, jaguars, pecarís, deer and mountain lions. There is also a wide variety of reptiles, including turtles, iguanas, snakes, lizards as well as of birds and fish, which abound along the coast and in estuaries of the rivers. Among the endangered species in 2004 there were 190 types of amphibians, 57 types of birds, 72 types of mammals, 106 types fish and 21 types of reptiles.

1.2   Ecosystems in Mexico: Forests, jungles and deserts

Mexico is among the countries with the greatest biodiversity on the planet, and it owes a large part of that biodiversity to the forests. This natural wealth is mirrored in the multiple cultures which have created social, cultural and artistic behaviour to adapt to the ecosystem.

Of all Mexican territory which is still covered by forests (ranked tenth in the world), half is temperate forest and the other half tropical forest or jungle.

Half of Mexican territory is covered by deserts, consisting of sand dunes, stony areas, thickets of various kinds, grasslands and forests. Deserts in the northwest, such as the Altar, are the driest in Mexico. In northern and central parts of the country the big sierras prevent rain reaching the deserts of the highlands and the Tehuacán valley. Mexico has the widest variety of reptiles in the world; it ranks second in variety of mammals and fourth in amphibians and plants. In addition, Mexico's pine-oak forests are the most diverse in the world, home to 55 species of pine (85% of which are endemic) and 138 of oak (70% endemic). Two thirds of the water consumed is collected from the forests and jungles of the country. Every year this ecosystem generates an amount of water that equals approximately 11 times the water of Lake Chapala, Mexico's largest (5,127.43km²) lake.

The Oyamel (Abies religiosa), a conifer of the family of Pinaceas, is a beautiful species of tree, proponent in providing a sanctuary for the Monarch butterfly and being the lungs of the largest city in the world, Mexico.

1.3 Communities and their relationship with forests

Peasants and indigenous people profit from much of Mexico's biodiversity, since 80% of the forests and jungles of this country belong to small farming cooperatives (ejidos) and communities. 10 million people currently inhabit these ecosystems, of which at least 5 million are indigenous.

- Two thirds of the Mexican people who live in forests are poor and depend on forest resources for their livelihood.
- They use their surroundings for food, medicines, construction materials and fuel (wood).
- Several communities make use of the forests without destroying them, because of their high cultural and spiritual value. For them using the forest is not a business but part of their cultural heritage.
- Under the conditions prevailing in the Mexican forests, the preservation, reforestation and sustainable use of natural resources is crucial.

- In some communities the controlled commercial use of the forests has helped preserve them, while in others it has caused social and ecological deterioration.
- In the "Regiones de Refugio" (Sanctuaries) conservation has never been a problem but it will still be necessary to adapt to the new conditions for sustainability.

The second half of the twentieth century was a crucial time of transition for Mexican peasant communities. The agrarian reform was not implemented with forest conservation in mind. Instead the experiences of the communities were ignored, and a contrary policy was adopted. These policies followed two general lines: overlapping the rights of use and a failure to recognize the sanctity of certain areas of forest.

Use rights were granted to external agents to use the resources of the forest even at the expense of the communities, i.e. forests with greater commercial potential, located in relatively more accessible areas, becoming subject to logging concessions.

1.4 Small farming cooperatives (Ejidos).
Certification of forest Management

A central feature of the small farming cooperatives and communities is their form of organization and communal land. The highest authority in the organizational structure of the cooperatives and communities is the assembly, which lays down the rules, elects the representatives and takes operational decisions. In some towns this structure has facilitated the process of certification of forest management, but in other cases it has been unfavorable because the representatives have not always helped the process. The cooperatives have large sawmills, nurseries, extraction equipment and activities aimed at making handling more efficient and therefore more profitable. This is not the case with smaller coops which do not have the financial resources and therefore invest in different activities.[2]

---

[2] Merino, Leticia; Bosques y Selvas; Reflexión en torno a su manejo y conservación; Instituto de Investigaciones Sociales; UNAM

In Mexico, certification is granted by the Rainforest Alliance organization, in collaboration with the Consejo Civil Mexicano para la Silvicultura Sustentable A.C. (CCMSS), who through the SmartWood Program (SW), credits the certification before the Forest Stewardship Council (FSC). Thus, CCMSS evaluates forest management (environmental, social and economic aspects of forest exploitation) of the producers, as well as the businesses involved in the production process, ensuring they comply with the principles and criteria established by the FSC and the rules of the SW program. Those who receive certification have the FSC logo on their products, which informs the consumer that the article comes from good forest management.

The certification of forest management began in Mexico in 1995. By November 2002, 67 candidates had been evaluated, 36 certificates had been awarded (22 to ejidos, nine to communities and nine to private entities). The 36 licenses granted to forest management add up to 613,671 ha, which accounts for 20% of the total area recognized.

The cooperatives and communities that have received certification can be found in Chihuahua, Durango, Michoacán, Oaxaca and Quintana Ro; states which together possess 40% of the total forested area. The Forest Inventory of Mexico has recorded 63,611,900 ha of wooded area (INE 2002), 50.3% in the temperate forests of conifers and 28.6% in the tropical forests. These same states reported managing 1,147,601ha of forest in October 2002, which accounted for 38.6% of the total forest managed in Mexico (2,975,854 ha). Most representatives of the cooperatives believe that if granted certification:

- Their communities serve as a role model in the development and dissemination of alternative forest management.
- They get publicity in markets that view forest management favourably
- It helps resolve internal conflicts, mainly in organization and allocation of profits
- Small businesses emerge which utilize the leftover wood, generate employment, and in other cases explore the possibilities of providing environmental services.

145

2. Current Situation

2.1 Deforestation

Mexico has one of the highest rates of deforestation in the world, losing an area of forest equivalent to 52,800 m² each year. The problems experienced by Mexico's forests are serious and need urgent attention.[3] The facts are grim:

- If the pace of deforestation in Mexico remains constant, the forests will have disappeared within the next sixty years.
- This will be an enormous loss because Mexico currently ranks eleventh in the world as regards forest cover.
- Already the diversity of reptiles, mammals, amphibians and plants is on the decline.
- This decline leads to the decline of those communities that for generations have made non-destructive use of the forest, which was considered part of their heritage.
- The problem affects not only local people, because the forests provide three quarters of all Mexican drinking water.
- Forests also stabilize regional climate; on a planetary scale they protect against climate change.
- Nevertheless, a policy of compulsory land clearing in order to expand grazing and cultivation has been strongly promoted.
- In addition, illegal logging has damaged the timber market.
- It cannot be denied that illegal logging and the absence of appreciation for the forest have marginalized the forest communities. The reason for this however, is to be found in policies that for decades have encouraged indiscriminate logging and land clearing, meaning the destruction of forests for arable land or pasture (82 percent of deforestation is due to this).
- For many years the Mexican pine forests, like those of other conifers, have been endangered due to the use of pine as timber and firewood.
- The ignorance as regards the importance of conserving the forests, especially when dealing with new strategies for exploiting resources such as: overgrazing, irresponsible exploitation of

---

[3] Greenpeace México; http://greenpeace.org/mexico

economically useful plants and ornamental plants, deforestation in order to provide pasture, uncontrolled hunting of large mammals, over-extraction of groundwater, mining, especially for construction materials, urbanization, waste and toxic materials, the irresponsible use of off-road vehicles and tourism.

The effective conservation of biodiversity requires the establishment, consolidation and maintenance of Natural Protected Areas and sustainable management schemes, addressing among other items the safeguarding of Mexican species of flora and fauna in danger of extinction.

2.2 Diverse public and private interests

The diverse facets of forest resources range from the provision of services for the public, such as environmental services and communal services, to private services such as the production of goods. While private interest emphasizes the loss of productive capacity, public interest concentrates more on the loss of the ability of the forest to carry out its environmental functions. Social interest is concerned with the deterioration of social capital in the peasant communities and their consequent poverty, dislocation and uprooting.

After only a few years the administration of the communal forestry company and its distribution of profits provoked criticism – in some communities it was argued that the communal authorities mishandled communal funds. The conflict acerbated and became violent. Forestry was suspended because the comuneros complained that the administration of the companies was corrupt and allowed a greater amount of logging than originally granted by Semarnap[4]. Since then the official logging has been suspended in some towns and coops, while at the same time clandestine logging has intensified.

Therefore it is imperative that regional and international conservation and development are generated through:

---

[4] Secretaría de medio ambiente, recursos naturales y pesca, México. Actualmente: SEMARNAT, Secretaria del medio ambiente y recursos naturales

- government agencies,
- NGOs,
- academic institutions and
- local communities,

in order to ensure conservation activities to preserve the biosphere.

3. Mexican National Parks

3.1 Natural Protected Areas

The Natural Protected Areas are legally defined in environmental policy to be used for the conservation of the environment, be it general as in the protection of biodiversity or specific as in the protection of an endangered species.

Forests and jungles

Forests cover 64.5 million hectares in Mexico, accounting for 33% of the national territory. These forests have a wide biodiversity, provide numerous economic benefits and are critical to the well-being of many communities, as a repository of ancient knowledge about the use of natural resources.

National Parks

National parks will be formed of one or more ecosystems that stand out for their scenic beauty, their scientific, educational, recreational or historical value, for their wildlife, their suitability for tourism development, or for other reasons of similar general interest.

Deserts

Deserts, with extreme temperatures in summer and sub-zero temperatures in winter extend through the states of Chihuahua, Coahuila, Sonora, Durango, Nuevo Leon, Tamaulipas and Zacatecas.

The rapid destruction of forests, jungles and deserts has endangered a wide variety of flora and fauna that are part of this ecosystem.

In Mexico, the main cause of deforestation is clearance to create pasture or arable land. This practice has been promoted by all levels of government, which have so far considered forests, jungles and deserts as idle land, unable to appreciate their many benefits.

3.2 Ordinance creation

National Parks are created by presidential decree and activities that can be carried out there are stipulated in the "General Law of Ecological Balance and Environmental Protection".

The National Commission of Protected Natural Areas currently administrates 161 natural areas of federal holding, a total of 227,128km², equivalent to 11.56% of the Mexican territory.

The National Program for Natural Protected Areas 2007-2012 regulates the following:

- Tourism in Protected Areas.
- Conservation Strategy for Development.
- Conservation of endangered species.

Between January and July 2007 three decrees were issued, in which three new natural protected areas (PNA) were established, totaling an area of 673,492 hectares. In January 2007 the following National Parks and Protected Areas were listed:

Área natural protegida	Decreto de creación	Sup. en ha.	Ubicación	Municipios	Ecosistemas
Constitución de 1857	27-04-62	5,009	Baja California	Ensenada.	Bosque de pino-encino y chaparral.
Sierra de San Pedro Mártir	26-04-47	72,911	Baja California	Ensenada.	Pinos, *abies, libocedrus, pseudotsuga*, chaparral.
Bahía de Loreto	19-07-96	206,581	Baja California Sur	Loreto.	Asociaciones de manglares y matorral espinoso, dunas costeras, matorral xerófilo.
Cabo Pulmo	06-06-95	7,111	Baja California Sur	Frente Municipio Los Cabos.	Arrecife coralino.
Los Novillos	18-06-40	42	Coahuila	Acuña.	Nogales, sauces y álamos.
Cañón del Sumidero	08-12-80	21,789	Chiapas	Tuxtla Gutiérrez, Soyalo, Osumacinta, San Fernando y Chiapa de Corzo.	Selva mediana subcaducifolia y baja caducifolia, encinar, pastizal.
Lagunas de Montebello	16-12-59	6,022	Chiapas	La Trinitaria y La Independencia	Bosque de pino, encino y mesófilo de montaña.
Palenque	20-07-81	1,772	Chiapas	Palenque.	Selva alta perennifolia y pastizal inducido.
Cascada de Bassaseachic	02-02-81	5,803	Chihuahua	Ocampo.	Bosque de pino y encino, encino, matorral xerófilo y pastizal.
Cumbres de Majalca	01-09-39	4,772	Chihuahua	Chihuahua.	Bosque de pino, encino, pino-encino, pastizal y matorral xerófilo.
Cerro de la Estrella	24-08-38	1,100	Distrito Federal	Iztapalapa.	Bosque artificial con eucalipto y cedro.
Cumbres del Ajusco	23-09-36	920	Distrito Federal	Tlalpan.	Bosque de pino, oyamel y páramo de altura.
Desierto de los Leones	27-11-17	1,529	Distrito Federal	Cuajimalpa y Álvaro Obregón.	Bosque de oyamel, pino-encino y garrya.
El Tepeyac	18-02-37	1,500	Distrito Federal	Gustavo A. Madero.	Bosque artificial de eucalipto y cedro.
Fuentes Brotantes de Tlalpan	28-09-36	129	Distrito Federal	Tlalpan.	Reforestación inducida
El Histórico Coyoacán	26-09-38	584	Distrito Federal	Coyoacán.	Reforestación de cedros, eucaliptos y otras.
Lomas de Padierna	22-04-38	670	Distrito Federal	Magdalena Contreras y Álvaro Obregón.	Reforestación de cedros
El Veladero	17-07-80	3,617	Guerrero	Acapulco de Juárez.	Selva baja caducifolia.
General Juan N. Álvarez	30-05-64	528	Guerrero	Chilapa de Álvarez.	Bosque de pino-encino
Grutas de Cacahuamilpa	23-04-36	1,600	Guerrero	Pilcaya y Taxco de Alarcón.	Selva baja caducifolia
El Chico	06-07-82	2,739	Hidalgo	Mineral Del Chico y Pachuca.	Bosque de oyamel y encino, pino-encino, cedro y pastizal.
Los Mármoles (Comprende Barranca de San Vicente y Cerro de Cangando)	08-09-36	23,150	Hidalgo	Jacala de Ledezma, Zimapan y Nicolás Flores.	Bosque de pino-encino y matorral xerófilo.
Tula	27-05-81	100	Hidalgo	Tula de Allende.	Matorral xerófilo.
Nevado de Colima	05-11-36	9,600	Colima	Cuauhtémoc y Comala.	Bosque de pino, oyamel y encino, pastizal alpino y matorral inerme.
Bosencheve	01-08-40	10,432	México y Michoacán	México: Villa de Allende y Villa Victoria. Michoacán: Zitácuaro.	Bosque de pino y oyamel.
Desierto del Carmen o Nixcongo	10-10-42	529	México	Tenancingo.	Bosque de pino, encino y cedro.

Insurgente Miguel Hidalgo y Costilla	18-09-36	1,580	México y Distrito Federal	Mexico: Ocoyoacac y Huixquilucan. Distrito Federal: Cuajimalpa	Bosque de oyamel y pino.
Iztaccihuatl - Popocatepelt	08-11-35	90,284	México, Puebla y Morelos	Mexico: Chalco, Tlalmanalco, Amecameca, Atlauta, Ixtapaluca, Texcoco y Ecatzingo. Puebla: Tlahuapan, Tianguismanalco, Calpan, Atlixco, Chiautzingo, Huejotzingo, San Felipe Teotlalcingo, San Salvador El Verde, San Nicolás de Los Ranchos y Tochimilco. Morelos: Tetela del Volcán. Tlaxcala: Nanacamilpa de Mariano Arista y Calpulalpan.	Bosque de pino y páramo de altura y zacatonal.
Los Remedios	15-04-38	400	México	Naucalpan de Juárez.	Bosque artificial de eucalipto.
Molino de Flores Nezahualcóyotl	05-11-37	49	México	Texcoco.	Ahuehuetes y bosque artificial de eucalipto, pirul, casuarina y fresno
Nevado de Toluca	25-01-36	46,784	México	Texcaltitlán, Toluca, Zinacantepec, Almoloya de Juárez, Amanalco, Temascaltepec, Coatepec Harinas, Villa Guerrero, Calimaya, Tenango Del Valle y Villa Victoria.	Bosque de oyamel, pino, zacatonal y páramo de altura.
Sacromonte	29-08-39	45	México	Amecameca.	Bosque artificial de encino, eucalipto, fresno y cedro.
Barranca del Cupatitzio	02-11-38	362	Michoacán	Uruapan.	Bosque de pino, pino-encino.
Cerro de Garnica	05-09-36	968	Michoacán	Hidalgo y Queréndaro.	Bosque de pino y oyamel.
Insurgente José Maria Morelos	22-02-39	4,325	Michoacán	Charo y Tzitzio	Bosque de pino, matorral y pastizal.
Lago de Camécuaro	08-03-41	10	Michoacán	Tangancícuaro.	Bosque de galería, ahuehuetes y sauce.
Pico de Tancítaro	27-07-40	23,154	Michoacán	Tancítaro, Nuevo Parangaricutiro, Peribán y Uruapan	Bosque de oyamel, pino y encino, pastizal y matorral.
Rayon	29-08-52	25	Michoacán	Tlalpujahua.	Bosque artificial de cedro y eucalipto.
Lagunas de Zempoala	27-11-36	4,790	Morelos y México	Morelos: Huitzilac. México: Ocuilan	Bosque de oyamel, pino y encino.
El Tepozteco	22-01-37	23,259	Morelos, y D. F.	Morelos: Tepoztlán. Distrito Federal: Milpa Alta.	Bosque de pino, oyamel, encino, selva baja caducifolia.
Isla Isabel	08-12-80	194	Nayarit	Santiago Ixcuintla.	Selva baja caducifolia, vegetación de dunas costeras.
Cumbres de Monterrey	17-11-00	177,396	Nuevo León	Allende, García, Montemorelos, Monterrey, Rayones, Santa Catarina, Santiago y San Pedro Garza García.	Bosque de pino encino, matorral xerófilo y pastizales
El Sabinal	25-08-38	8	Nuevo León	Cerralvo.	Bosque de galería.
Huatulco	24-07-98	11,891	Oaxaca	Santa Maria Huatulco.	Selva baja caducifolia, vegetación riparia, humedales, manglares, ambiente marino con bancos de coral, algas y pastos marinos.
Benito Juárez	30-12-37	2,737	Oaxaca	Oaxaca de Juarez, San Andrés Huayapam, San Pablo Etla y San Agustín Etla.	Bosque de pino y encino, selva baja caducifolia.
Lagunas de Chacahua	09-07-37	14,187	Oaxaca	San Pedro Tututepec.	Selva mediana perennifolia y baja caducifolia, manglar y vegetación de dunas costeras.
Cerro de Las Campanas	07-07-37	58	Querétaro	Querétaro.	Reforestación de eucalipto.
El Cimatario	21-07-82	2,448	Querétaro	Querétaro, Corregidora y Huimilpan.	Matorral xerófilo.

151

Arrecifes de Cozumel	19-07-96	11,988	Quintana Roo	Cozumel.	Arrecife coralino.
Arrecife de Puerto Morelos	02-02-98	9,067	Quintana Roo	Benito Juárez.	Arrecife coralino
Costa Occidental de Isla Mujeres, Punta Cancún y Punta Nizuc	19-07-96	8,673	Quintana Roo	Isla Mujeres y Benito Juárez.	Arrecife coralino
Isla Contoy	02-02-98	5,126	Quintana Roo	Isla Mujeres.	Manglar, selva baja caducifolia, coctal, zona costera y halófitas
Tulum	23-04-81	664	Quintana Roo	Felipe Carrillo Puerto.	Selva mediana, manglar y vegetación de dunas costeras.
Arrecifes de Xcalak	27-11-00	17,949	Quintana Roo	Othon P. Blanco	Arrecifes de coral
Gogorrón	22-09-36	25,000	San Luis Potosí	Villa de Reyes.	Bosque de pino-encino, matorral xerófilo.
El Potosí	15-09-36	2,000	San Luis Potosí	Río Verde.	Bosque de pino, encino y pastizal.
Malinche o Matlalcuéyatl	06-10-38	45,711	Tlaxcala y Puebla	Tlaxcala: Ixtenco, Chiautempan, Huamantla, Teolocholco, Zitlaltepec de Trinidad Sánchez Santos, Tzompantepec, Mazateocochco de José María Morelos, Acuamanala de Miguel Hidalgo, Contla de Juan Cumatzi, San Pablo Del Monte y Tlaxcala Puebla: Amozoc, Puebla, Acajete y Tepatlaxco de Hidalgo.	Bosque pino-encino, oyamel y zacatonal.
Xicoténcatl	17-11-37	680	Tlaxcala	Tlaxcala.	Reforestación ornamental
Cañon del Río Blanco	22-03-38	55,690	Veracruz	Orizaba, Chocaman, Fortin, Ixtaczoquitlan, Atzacan, Nogales, Camerino Z. Mendoza, Maltrata, Aquila, Rio Blanco, Rafael Delgado, Acultzingo, Soledad Atzompa, Naranjal y Huilopan de Cuauhtémoc.	Selva mediana perennifolia, bosque de pino y mesófilo de montaña.
Cofre de Perote	04-05-37	11,700	Veracruz	Perote, Xico, Ayahualulco y Acajete.	Bosque de pino y oyamel.
Pico de Orizaba	04-01-37	19,750	Veracruz y Puebla	Puebla: Tlachichuca, Chalchicomula de Sesma y Atzitzintla. Veracruz: Calcahualco y La Perla.	Bosque de pino, oyamel, encino, aile.
Sistema Arrecifal Veracruzano	24-08-92	52,239	Veracruz	Frente A Veracruz, Boca Del Río y Alvarado.	Arrecife coralino y vegetación halófita.
Arrecife Alacranes	06-06-94	333,769	Yucatán	Frente Al Municipio de Progreso.	Arrecife coralino.
Dzibilchantun	14-04-87	539	Yucatán	Mérida.	Selva baja caducifolia.
Sierra de Órganos	27-11-00	1,125	Zacatecas	Sombrerete	
Islas Marietas	25-04-05	1,383	Nayarit	Bahía de Banderas	
Archipiélago de San Lorenzo	25-04-05	58,442	Baja California	Frente a las costas de Ensenada (Golfo de California)	
Archipiélago Espíritu Santo	10-05-07	48,655	Baja California Sur	La Paz	

Figure 1: The National Parks and Protected Areas of Mexico[5]

---

[5] Consejo Nacional de Áreas Protegidas. México: http://www.conanp.gob.mx

4. Tourism and ecosystems

The National Development Plan 2007-2012, provides for the creation of a responsible and intelligent management of Mexico's natural resources, and promotes environmental sustainability.

It aims to ensure environmental sustainability with Mexicans in the care, protection, preservation and rational exploitation of the natural wealth of the country, without compromising natural heritage and quality of life for future generations.

4.1 Sustainable Tourism

It is evident that in recent years tastes have changed and more non-conventional forms of tourism have emerged. The emphasis is on more active and participatory tourism, interaction with nature projecting new concerns and profiles of tourists who are more informed, committed and aware of their natural and cultural environment (Burkart y Medlik; Mathieson 1990).

Correspondingly, the market segment in tourism that revolves around nature has grown and in its wake follow concepts, banding together nature and tourism, under names like ecotourism, nature tourism, green tourism, alternative tourism and sustainable tourism, amongst others.

There are still a number of conflicting views concerning sustainability some contradictory in themselves, each trying to impose what they think is the best definition of this development.

4.2 Tourism in Protected Areas of Mexico

Mexico has the best natural and cultural settings for a wide range of activities. The tourist can experience the excitement of adventure tourism and eco-tourism, enjoy exclusive luxury tourism, relax on sunny beaches and discover the culture and entertainment that is unique to Mexico.

Tourism as a state policy is implemented in programs that contribute to a balanced and sustainable growth of activity in protected areas. These activities include: rock climbing, hiking, excursions, paragliding, mountain biking and diving.

5.   Contribution of tourism to National Parks

5.1   Benefit for national parks

Tourism can benefit National Parks in the following way:

- It is the aim that through the creation of National Parks the situation for the communities in those areas shall be improved.
- Strengthening sustainability requires comprehensive planning, ordering and managing the development of social and productive activities such as ecotourism.
- Ecotourism will be advanced by thinking and working across regional borders. In this way the economic development of villages, the protection of the natural reserves as well as of biodiversity can be taken care of.
- The development of the local eco-tourism-industry will be supported, advancing the general standard of living by putting local people in charge and involving them in the planning and implementation of projects.
- Employers will have an opportunity to pool their efforts to promote sustainable tourism.
- Amongst the benefits is also an opportunity to bring about a change of spending patterns in the tourists.

5.2   Participation of society

Essential elements of sustainable tourism are the involvement of the community and that its development is aimed at reconciling tourism and nature, its core concern being the welfare of both tourists and the host community. This allows communities to realize all the benefits they can receive, and makes cultural interaction between tourists and the native people possible.

In recent years, the authorities have made their policy more social, more environmentally sustainable and economically more profitable, placing great importance on social participation.

5.3 The Secretary of Tourism (SECTUR)

The Ministry of Tourism considers alternative tourism as an opportunity to extend the range of tourism products in Mexico and consolidate a model of sustainable development. It therefore has established a work-program in order to strengthen this sector through strategies of Technology Transfer.

The Federal Law on Tourism states: Areas identified by the Ministry of Tourism for their natural, historical or cultural monuments constitute a tourist attraction.

The Ministry of Tourism, with its the strategy of Development and Technology Transfer, aims to guide, facilitate and unify criteria for the establishment of tourism products within the frame of sustainability and competition.

In tourism products, tourists can enjoy horseback riding, extreme sports, natural landscapes; barbecue huts and antojito bars and observe a variety of animals.

6. Future Trends

To achieve the above, the SECTUR has set the following goals for the period of 2007 - 2012, as part of its Nature Tourism Program:

- The creation of 60 Natural Protected Areas under the Nature Tourism Development Program with an emphasis on sustainability and competitiveness.
- The creation of 40 Natural Protected Areas having infrastructure and equipment for the development of activities in Nature Tourism.
- Diversification activities in 30 of the main beach resorts and inland destinations, by offering eco- and adventure tourism.
- An 80% increase in domestic suppliers specializing in Nature Tourism, mainly operated by rural or indigenous groups.
- Incorporating community groups as micro-entrepreneurs to generate sources of employment, providing a territorial foothold and promoting local development.
- Positioning Mexico at international level as a travel destination for ecotourism.

Its main objectives (2007 - 2012) are to:

- Increase the number of tourists involved in cultural tourism to 50%.
- Consolidate 9 World Heritage Cities.
- Consolidate 9 archeological heritage sites.
- Include 50 `Magic Villages´ into the tourist destinations.
- Increase the number of monuments and archaeological sites as tourist attractions.
- Develop overlapping public policies on culture and tourism.
- Local planning, including development plans for urban centers with the focus on tourism.
- Management of the cultural heritage associated with tourism.
- Incorporation of intangible heritage to the attractiveness of tourist destinations of Mexico.
- Generating cultural industries as an input into tourism destinations.
- Execution of cultural activities linking the private sector to tourism.
- Competitive tourism products that value the Mexican culture as a whole and at the same time strengthen the local cultures.

Because it is based on the particularities of each destination or municipality, specific actions should be implemented in the quest to identify and generate competitive advantage, which requires the definition of a long-term strategy. This will be achieved by designing a portfolio of each tourist destination, to emphasize its core competencies and create favourable environments.

7. Conclusions

Mexico has without a doubt great resources in its forests and deserts. These provide a wide range of options for regional development of the areas with outstanding forest management and agricultural activities, carried out by authorized farmers and communities.

The myriad actions against ecosystems have been highlighted, which have led to a deterioration and/or loss of large tracts of them, causing an imbalance in the environment and further degradation of the economic and social stability of the different regions of Mexico.

The process of finding solutions to either maintain or regain this balance, has led to sustainable tourism, in an effort to strengthen the ties between society and nature.

The wise use of protected areas in Mexico, the introduction of eco or green tourism will increase the awareness of our duty to preserve natural protected areas.

The involvement of the Ministry of Tourism is vitally important, as an intermediary institution between community and tourists, which with its goals and objectives, proposes establishing a viable and realistic way to ensure that the development and growth of nature tourism benefits society. However, without the selfless and active participation of society, all efforts would be in vain and the process of deterioration and loss would continue.

References

Vargas Márquez, Fernando. (1984). *Parques Nacionales de México y Reservas Equivalentes. Pasado, presente y futuro. Colección: Grandes Problemas de Nacionales. Serie: Los Bosques de México. Instituto de Investigaciones Económicas.* UNAM. México, D.F.

Comisión Nacional de Áreas Naturales Protegidas. *CONANP.* http://www.conanp.gob.mx

SAG. (1970). *Código Forestal. Subsecretaría Forestal y de la Fauna.* Departamento de Divulgación.

SAG. (1936-1968). *Expedientes del archivo económico de los parques nacionales.*

Hernández Granados, Gracia. (1977). *Estudio geográfico histórico de Iztapalapa. Colegio de Geografía. Facultad de Filosofía y Letras.* UNAM. México, D.F.

Dirección de Áreas Naturales Protegidas. (1996). *Archivos oficiales de los parques nacionales. SEMARNAP. INE. UCANP. Subdirección de Protección y Desarrollo. Departamento de Parques Nacionales.* http://semarnat.gob.mx

SARH. (1993). *Diagnóstico del Parque Nacional Bosencheve, Estado de México. Subsecretaría Forestal y de Fauna Silvestre. Consultores en Ecología y Medio Ambiente.*

Luna Montoya, José Luis. (2007). *Los Parque Nacionales de México. Ponencia.* Universidad Anáhuac, México Norte.

Lorenzo, José Luis. (1964). *Los Glaciares de México. Monografías del Instituto de Geofísica. Segunda Edición. Informe que rinde la Sección de Galciología del Comité Nacional de México para el año Geofísico Internacional.*

González, Ambrosio y Víctor Manuel Sánchez L. (1961). *Los Parques nacionales de México. Situación actual y problemas. Instituto Mexicano de Recursos Naturales Renovables.* México. D.F.

Greenpeace México. http://greenpeace.org/mexico

Graciela Cruz Jiménez. *Ecoturismo y Turismo Sustentable;* UAEM. México.

Hernández Macías, H. (2006). *La vida en los desiertos mexicanos. Colección: La Ciencia para Todos. Fondo de Cultura Económica,* México, D.F.

Merino Pérez, Leticia (2003). *Reflexiones en torno a su manejo y conservación. Instituto de Investigaciones Sociales,* Universidad Nacional Autónoma de México.

Hernández Macías, H. (2006). *La vida en los desiertos mexicanos. Colección: La Ciencia para Todos 213. Fondo de Cultura Económica.*

"México (república)," Enciclopedia Microsoft® Encarta® Online 2007. *http://mx.encarta.msn.com © 1997-2007 Microsoft Corporation. Reservados todos los derechos.*

National Parks and Tourism in China

Xu Honggang & Wolfgang Georg Arlt

1. The National Park system in China

There is no unified National Park system in China. In China, National Parks are sorted into different forms which are under the jurisdiction of different political bodies:

- The Scenic Parks - Construction Ministry
- The Natural Reserves - Environmental Protection Administration (EPA) and Forestry Ministry
- The Geo-parks - Land Ministry
- The National Forest Parks - Forestry Ministry

Very few National Parks were established in China before the 1980s; however, many have been created since. Up to 2004, there were 226 National Reserves in China, about 8.86% of the national land area. This is greater than the global average.

1.1 Scenic Parks

Among these, Scenic Parks are considered to be similar to the National Parks defined by UNESCO. The target of the Scenic Park was to provide opportunities for the people to appreciate and enjoy the cultural and natural landscape. The first 44 national Scenic Parks were established in 1982. Before 2004, 133 national Scenic Parks and 452 provincial Scenic Parks were established. The total area of the Scenic Parks was about 1% of the national territory (Qiu 2007).

The Scenic Park system contains the most famous scenic resources around China. Most of the Scenic Parks are in the east and middle region of China. Within the Scenic Park system, the National Scenic Park system is the most important part of it. By 2005, there existed 177 national level Scenic Parks and 452 provincial level Scenic Parks.

161

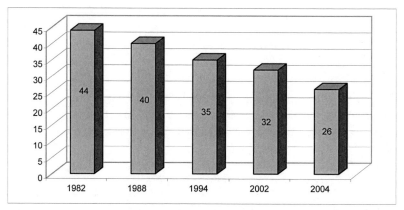

Fig. 1: The establishment of the Scenic Parks (National level) between 1982-2004[1]

The value of the Scenic Park lies in the fact that it is a cultural landscape. The most important issues involved here are Preservation, Sightseeing and Recreation. A famous example of a national Scenic Park is the Yellow Mountain Huangshan. The importance of the cultural aspects of the national Scenic Parks were recognized by the international world and UNESCO even created a new category of world heritage sites, natural-cultural dual heritage titles for Chinese famous mountains when Taishan Mountain applied to world heritage

1.2 Natural Reserves

China has established a considerable number and size of the Natural Reserves system. The earliest was in Guangdong, in 1956. Similar to other parks or protected areas, there are three categories of Natural Reserves:

- National ones,
- provincial ones and
- county ones.

---

[1] Source: Own presentation after Qiu 2007

National Natural Reserves are the most important part of this system. Natural Reserves System covers the typical ecosystems in China, and lays a firm foundation for the biodiversity protection. Most National Natural Reserves are in the western part of China, where the ecological environment is more fragile and the economy is underdeveloped. Most of the lands of Nature Reserves are in the hand of Forestry Ministry and jointly managed by the Forestry Ministry and the EPA. In the mission of Natural Reserve, the protection of the biodiversity is at the highest priority.

The planning model for Nature Reserves is based on the distinction between Core zone, buffer area and development zone. As the emphasis is on the protection of the area, this model is not welcomed in some underdeveloped region, where development is seen as more important than protection for the current generation. Without tourism income, the Natural Reserves would have difficulties to finance the operational and maintenance costs.

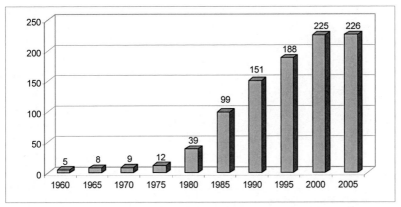

Fig. 2: Accumulated number of National Nature Reserve 1960-2005[2]

1.3 National Forest Parks

The main reason for the establishment of the Forest Parks is the restriction of logging. The first national Forestry Park was established in Zhangjiajie in 1982. Here the emphasis is not too strict on protection,

---

[2] Source: Own presentation after Qiu 2007

but focusing on the recreation. The pressure on the forests parks to sustain the staffs is high. The Forest Parks therefore target at the recreational and resort tourists to increase their income.

1.4 Geo-parks

Geo-parks are the newcomers among the National Parks in China. The first geological park was setup in 2001 only, but up to 2004, there were already 85 national geo-parks in China. This number grew to 138 in 2005, among them 12 World Geo Parks. Since the Geo-parks are the new comers, some are overlapping with the other Scenic Parks and Natural Reserves.

2. Tourism development in the National Parks

Domestic tourism in China developed strongly since the mid-1980s. In 1991 about 300 million trips were counted, in 2004 already the 1 billion mark was passed. Today statistically every citizen of the People's Republic of China goes on more than one trip per year (CNTA 2008). Nature and Heritage tourism were officially acknowledged with the National Heritage Conservation Act of 1982 and the beginning of larger numbers of National Park designations (Arlt/Job 2006).

National Parks are the most important undertaker of natural tourism. National Parks are considered as economic engine for many regions, especially in underdeveloped regions. They are also important drivers for urbanization as can be seen from the examples of Wuyishan and Huangshan. The National Parks are major financial contributors for the regions because these regions are "gate economy". The substantial tourism income is from the tickets.

The economic and social multiplier effects of National Parks have shown to be limited. But because of the overuse and uneven distribution of the tourists among the National Parks, with hotspots like Zhangjiajie and Huangshan receive up to two million visitors a year; the environmental stress is also high to these hot spot while the financial pressures are high for others. Even for these "hot-spot" tourism destinations with National Parks, economically "gate economy" or a "cable car economy" limit trickle-down effects. The social effects are not fully realized by the lack of understanding for the dual structure between the big park and the small surrounding communities and the multiple objectives of the National Parks, especially the educational value versus the entertainment value.

3. Studies of the National Parks

Most of the National Parks were established by the local governments of the less developed regions. While these National Parks provide opportunities for the preservation, of valuable resources, they are also perceived to be, and are used as, the drivers for regional development through the market economy system. Therefore, the National Parks in China are facing a more uncertain and complex situation than those in many other countries. Although it is well understood that social, economic and political factors ultimately determine the establishment, management and performance of the National Parks, limited empirical research has been conducted to systematically understand their complexity. There are a number of important questions connected to the National Parks system:

- Should the parks be mainly used to protect the nature or to be the economic drivers for local development?
- How to solve the conflicts between the local communities and the managers of the National Parks over enclave lands within the National Parks?
- How to solve the institutional problems, especially the overlapping of the institutions and their responsibilities and the dual management structure of the park with ministries and local governments involved, often with conflicting interests?
- How to overcome the current lack of R&D support? and
- How to overcome the separation of the culture from the natural landscape?

For Chinese tourism scholars, including the School of Tourism Management of the Sun Yat-sen University in Guangzhou, a number of research interests are connected with the studies of the National Parks:

- The institutional arrangement
- Carrying capacity
- The environmental protection

- Tourism planning
- Visitor management
- Pricing
- Community issues
- Market studies
- Resource based economic development

Two major themes on the studies of National Parks are discussed below. No attempt is made here at a comprehensive review of the literature. The discussion explores the perspectives of Chinese tourism research, their efforts, theory development and the constraints by presenting these two important themes. It only provides some contextual background of the tourism research on National Parks in China. The contextual background showed that there is no ready for use model which can be introduced to China to address these issues. However, long term efforts are need to understand the dynamics of the National Parks and the underlying structures on which polices can be recommended.

3.1 The institutional study of the National Parks

Since most of the National Parks were established in the transition period, the discussion on the institutional arrangement of National Parks became unavoidable when the institutional structure was found to be the key to determine the utilization and protection of the tourism resources and the distribution of the welfare among different groups, while achieving the goal of sustainable development at the same time.

In the planned economy era, there were a few national Scenic Parks. These were national cultural heritages which were owned and managed by the government (normally directly by the central government). In the transition period, the management right and the financial burden of the managing national resources were handed down to the local governments and a dual management structure was put into place. This decentralization process provides both opportunities and pressures for the locals to utilize and protect these valuable resources.

This tourism development of these parks could only be made possible when privatization was allowed because the local governments could not raise enough money for the infrastructure building and are also not allowed to participate in the business.

In China, not all the land is owned by the national government. When most of the National Parks were established, some of the land was still owned by the local communities living and cultivating inside the parks. These local communities also expect to use the resources for their benefits. The conflicts between the local communities and the local governments and the management companies therefore can be very intensive.

Yet, National Parks are still regarded as the National Property and as a public good. Environmental NGOs and national ministries still have right to intervene in the use and protection of the parks.

Overall, the decentralization and privatization increases the number of stakeholders. The governments, the public-owned enterprises, private companies, communities, tourists and other NGOs which have different agenda toward the parks can directly or indirectly affect the effectiveness of the management of these attractions. The dynamical conflicts among these stakeholders determine the status of the protection and utilization of the resources.

Theoretical and empirical studies have been carried out to debate the management model of National Parks (Wang 2002). On one hand, normative studies discuss how the institutional structure should be designed to achieve the sustainable development. The property rights, the management rights, the consumption rights of the National Parks and the proper allocation of the rights are discussed. Empirical studies on the other hand attempt to identify available patterns of institutional structure of tourism attractions nationwide, and to explore the relationship between the institutional structure and efficiency of the sustainable use of tourism attractions. The debates triggered by these studies are still going on.

3.2 The cultural factors influencing tourism in the National Parks

One major difference of the studies of the National Parks in China is the focus on the importance of cultural aspects of the National Parks. The studies have recognized that the long civilization in China has made deep impacts on Chinese landscape, including the Natural Reserves and natural areas. These impacts are not only made for the purpose of production and living but also because Chinese have a strong spiritual attachment to the nature.

The idea of unification between human and nature determines the landscape patterns in China. It is a common believe that men should not be perceived as being isolated from nature. The Fengshui model is used to select the place for houses and villages. A typical positive fengshui is seen as a place which is surrounded and protected by mountains on the north side and has a river running in the south. Temples and hermits houses are built inside the mountains where good fengshui are believed to be located. These temples are very integrated with nature and appear to be part of nature. There are therefore few mountains in China without temples and the development of traveling in the mountains was often first made for pilgrimages but is now also used for tourists (Xie 1995).

3.3 Place attachment: Experiencing the Scenic Parks

Chinese developed an appreciation for the nature very early. All the influential philosophers in China encourage people to go to the nature and learn from nature. In the writings of Kongzi (Confucius), scholars are always encouraged to go the nature to search for wisdom and spiritual enlightenment. His saying "Kind men enjoy mountains and wise men love water" is often quoted in China. Already in the Western Jin Dynasty (around 300 AD), Shanshui ("Mountain and water") poems flourished and continue till now. This was much earlier than the development of western poems and paintings which concentrate only on natural beauty.

Almost all the mountains have been described in these poems which have been taught for centuries. As the results, people on all levels of education have already developed a strong attachment to these places like Huangshan (Yellow Mountain) or Lushan. Chinese tourists also demonstrate a strong preference for familiar landscape through various images created through poets and artists.

In fact, it is very difficult to distinguish whether it is the landscape which brings the people or the famous poem which attracts people to these places. The attractions of the mountains and Scenic Places are not evaluated according to the natural beauty per se but according to the tangible and intangible cultural heritage embodied, especially to its connections with these famous people and famous poets. These poems and short couplets have also carved in big characters on special stones at the place centuries ago, creating a special tourism site. The quality of these couplets and poems play an extremely important role in the ranking of the natural sites. For instance, Tianlao Mountain became well known due to a poem by China's most famous poet Li Bai (701-762). Yueyanglou in Hunan Province was not seen as being of any importance until Fan Zhongyan (989-1052), a famous scholar in the Northern Song Dynasty wrote an essay memorizing the reconstruction of the building. This inseparable character of cultural heritage with nature has been acknowledged by UNESCO which invented the dual title of Cultural and Natural heritage for Chinese scenic mountains. The tradition for the Chinese to visit the places which are described by famous poets helps to explain the overcrowdedness of a few popular sites.

In the meanwhile, for many of the Chinese, the importance of the protection of the landscape is to reveal the image created by these poets, not really meaning to preserve the integrity of the nature itself or to protect the existing level of biodiversity. It can be said while Chinese have a systematic view toward nature and human, the interests and concerns for most of the people are still dominated by the cultural perspective.

The examination of the two themes demonstrates the potentials and richness of tourism studies related with the National Parks. Both topics have accumulated substantial knowledge and provide insights into Chinese tourism development phenomena. In addition, the studies of tourism at the National Parks can also reflect the key issues currently discussed in the academic world: local-global context, development and conservation, marketing planning, formal and informal sector, modernity and traditions. However, there are clear limitations of the current research, namely:

- A concentration of research topics
- The lack of integrated studies especially in the fields of Scientific research, Humanity and Management
- The lack of a long term vision of the National Park research: There is a problem solving orientation, but reactive approach not proactive approach. Many researchers are overwhelmed by the imported western theories and concepts. Yet it can be seen no western model and paradigm can be used directly in Chinese National Parks
- The need to build up a shared vision is not seen be all involved

4. The linkage of the school of tourism management of Sun Yat-sen University and National Parks

The School of Tourism Management is one of 26 schools in Sun Yat-sen University. It is established on the basis of the former Department of Tourism and Leisure. The City School of Tourism Management is located at the Zhuhai campus, which is about one and a half hour bus distance from Guangzhou City.

The school recruits undergraduates, postgraduates, and PhD students in hotel management, MICE management, tourism planning & destination management and leisure& sports management. National Park Management is within the program of tourism planning and destination management

With regard to National Parks, the school supported recently two PhD dissertations and a few master dissertations. It also finished a number of consulting projects, among them around 10 tourism plannings for the National Parks. Finally for industrial placements, cooperations are established with Zhangjiajie and Kanas National Park.

4.1 The technical supports to Kanas Parks

Lake Kanas is located in the north of the province Xinjiang in the Altai Mountains. It is a new attractions compared with the traditional Scenic Parks. It was "discovered" by the photography fans and then the values were gradually appreciated. Gradually, a national reserve, national Scenic Park, national geological park, and forestry park were setup. Some of these parks are overlapping with each other. As a result, it is difficult to develop an integrated tourism plan and there is a strong competition from various agencies for the development inside their area. On the other hand, despite the high time and money cost for visiting Kanas are high for Chinese, the tourist number grew rapidly. The risk for the resource misuse was high.

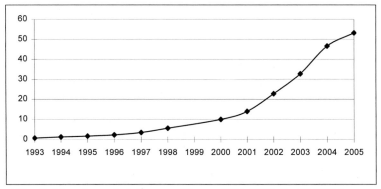

Fig. 3: Number of visitors to Kanas 1993-2005 (in 10,000)[3]

The Centre of Tourism Planning and Management was invited to carry out a tourism plan for this area. In order to plan for the most appropriate forms of tourism development for Lake Kanas Nature Reserve and surrounding areas, it is necessary to define as clearly as possible the range of issues that impact upon any decision making and which set the parameters and framework within which such planning can take place. Accordingly, following the field trip to Altai Prefecture on the Province of Xinjiang by a team of tourism planers from Zhongshan University in July 2005, the following list of key issues has been drawn up and aspects of each issue subjected to detailed scrutiny. During the research, a number of key issues could be identified:

- Differing perceptions of priorities for tourism
- Development by different stakeholders, resulting in the lack of a consensus vision for the future
- The need to identify core touristic values of the region and to translate them into appropriate forms of tourism development and activities
- Meeting the needs of communities in terms of tourism development
- The lack of integration between the core tourist areas of Kanas
- Impact of the Xinjiang/Russian Highway on potential tourism development

[3] Source: Own presentation, Data from: Kanas Management Bureau

- Lack of professional training and service delivery, and current ad hoc growth in core areas

The tourism planning team attempts to:

- Introducing a consultative approach to the community tourism planning
- Implementing a zoning strategy
- Proposal for establishing a National Park which covers the whole area of Nature Reserve, geological park, etc. One administrative office was setup to manage the whole area including the communities inside. Therefore conflicts on the resource usage can be solved
- Other training problems for the community and the local staff
- Possibility to restrict the tourist number through the road system development

The planning was supported by the local government. Efforts were made to integrate these fragmented institutions into one government institution which can facilitate the zoning strategy. In addition, a research cooperative agreement was reached between the local government and the school of tourism management which will keep on providing them the technical supports.

4.2 The R&D support to Zhangjiajie and Wulingyuan

Since 1982, when Zhangjiajie Forest Farm was officially approved to become the first national Forest Park, neighboring Wulingyuan was sequentially designated as National Park by the State Council, inscribed into the "World Heritage List" by UNESCO and identified as an AAAAA class scenic spot by the National Tourism Bureau, a National Geological Park by the Ministry of Land and Resources and a World Geological Park by the UNESCO. Both Zhangjiajie and Wulingyuan belong to the UNESCO world heritage, but remain two independent institutions competing for tourists. This UNESCO heritage site is a remarkable area. It can be viewed from the topics of the peaks looking down, from the bottom of the valleys looking up, and in the caverns underground.

The potential for tourism development has been recognized. World Cultural Heritage Site conveys immediate status as a place worth visiting to an international clientele. The tourism infrastructure is fully development. Airports and railways were built and connected to the major cities. Highways were also finished in 2006. Inside the park roads and cable cars were setup to transport thousands of tourists safely to viewpoints.

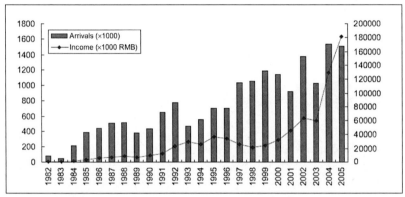

Fig. 4: Arrivals and income of the park 1982 to 2005[4]

Yet, problems are also accumulating with the rapid tourism development. The negative consequences on the tourism infrastructure building even caused the UNESCO to issue a warning flag to the world heritage site in 2004. These problems, including the environmental consequences and the social conflicts have already led the destination to enter a consolation stage of the development (Zhang/Xu, 2007, Zhong/Deng/Xiang 2007).

A partnership is currently built between Wulingyuan and the School of Tourism Management which provides continuous advices for the local governments for the sustainable tourism development. Currently, the research team is working mainly in the fields of traffic control of tourist flow, the community issue and development of ecotourism products for the hikers etc.

---

[4] Source: Zhangjiajie National Forest Park Administration 2006

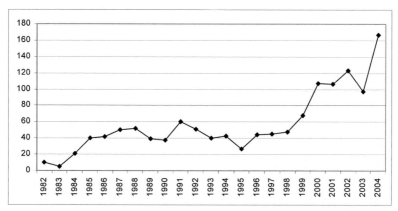

Fig. 5: Development of visitor numbers to Wulingyuan 1982-2004[5]

4.3   Potentials and problems with the cooperation

There remain a number of problems of the linkage between the tourism schools and National Parks:

- There is a rather low attractiveness of the National Parks to our students since most of students still prefer staying in the cities rather than in the remote places
- There is a lack of appreciation of research due to monopoly status of popular National Parks
- There is a lack of financial supports from the non-tourism hot spots although their interests
- There is still a tension between the short term objectives from the local stakeholders and the long term targets from the researchers. Local stakeholders are under pressure to maintain a high level of tourist arrival and the expectation of short term effects is high

---

[5] In 10,000, Source: Hang/Xu 2007

5.   Conclusion

The relationship between nature and human is the core of Chinese civilization. Chinese people have developed strong attachments to many of the National Parks. Therefore, studies on the tourism in the National Parks can help the understanding Chinese philosophy and culture which in turn also explain the unique patterns of domestic tourism to the National Parks in China.

One the other hand, most of the National Parks in China were established in the transition period from the planned to the market economy and from a centrally controlled to a locally driven system. This transition determines the competition for the control and use of the National Parks are high and the conflicts are increasing. Attempts have been made to explore and reach a balance between the conflicting goals in these parks. Some are successful and some not. Empirical researches and theoretical developments are both needed for developing good strategies for the sustainable use of the National Parks.

Overall, there are great potential for the two sides to get benefits from the cooperation. Although there is no tradition for National Parks to support universities to carry out researches, a good cooperation has started. It is expected that through a learning process, a reinforcing feedback which would benefit the two would be built.

Acknowledgement

This study was partially supported by the Chinese NSF (70503007)

References

Arlt, Wolfgang Georg, Job, Hubert: Introduction: Tourism and Sustainable Development in China. In: Job, H./Li, J.: *Natural Heritage, Ecotourism and Sustainable Development.* Regensburg 2006, 1-9.

CNTA.com (accessed May 22, 2008).

Qiu, B.X. (2007): *Implement the scientific model for development and promote a harmony development of Scenic Parks.* Presentation at the National Meeting on Implementation of National Regulation on Scenic Park, Beijing. 1 December.

Wang X. B. (2002): *The Reform of Managerial Modes of China's Natural and Culture Heritage.* Tourism Tribune. 2002. 17(5).

Xie L:G. (1995): *National Park Development in the World and Thinking about China Scenic Spot.* Urban and Village Construction. 8:24-26.

Zhang C.Z., Xu H.G.: *Institutional changes of World Heritage Management in China: Case Study of Wulingyuan.* Management World. 2007.8.

Zhong, L, et al.: *Tourism development and tourism area life cycle model: a case study of Zhangjiajie National Forest Park, China.* Tourism Management (2007).

Abkürzungsverzeichnis

ADFC	Allgemeiner Deutscher Fahrrad-Club e.V.
AIEST	Association internationale d'experts scientifiques du tourisme
APEIS	Asia-Pacific Environmental Innovation Strategies
AUbE	Akademie für Umweltforschung und -bildung in Europa
B.A.T.	British American Tobacco
BIS	Besucher-Informationssystem
BfN	Bundesamt für Naturschutz
BMU	Bundesministerium für Umwelt, Naturschutz und Reaktorsicherheit
BNatSchG	Bundesnaturschutzgesetz
CCMSS	Consejo Civil Mexicano para la Silvicultura Sustentable
CGE	Computable General Equilibrium
CNTA	China National Tourism Administration
CONANP	Comisión Nacional de Áreas Naturales Protegidas
CWSS	Common Wadden Sea Secretariat
DoC	Department of Conservation
dwif	Deutsches Wirtschaftswissenschaftliches Institut für Fremdenverkehr e.V.
DTV	Deutscher Tourismusverband e.V.
DZT	Deutsche Zentrale für Tourismus e.V.
EEZs	Exclusive Economic Zones
EMNID	Erforschung der öffentlichen Meinung, Marktforschung, Nachrichten, Informationen und Dienstleistungen
FHW	Fachhochschule Westküste
FIT	Free Independent Traveller
FÖNAD	Föderation der Natur- und Nationalparke Europas e.V.
FSC	Forest Stewardship Council
FTE	full-time equivalent
F.U.R	Forschungsgemeinschaft Urlaub und Reisen e.V.
GDP	Gross Domestic Product
GRNP	Gunung Rinjani National Park
GRNPP	Gunung Rinjani National Park Project
GSG	Großschutzgebiete
i.G.	in Gründung

IDRC	Indonesia International Development Research Centre
IMG	Investitions- und Marketinggesellschaft Sachsen-Anhalt mbH
IMT	Institut für Management und Tourismus
IUCN	International Union for Conservation of Nature
KMNK	Kantor Menteri Negara Kependudukan (Ministry of Population)
KONRAT	kommunale Nationalparkrat Jasmund
LMG	Landesmarketing Sachsen-Anhalt GmbH
LMO	Landesmarketingorganisation
LVwA	Landesverwaltungsamt
MARPOL	International Convention for the Prevention of Pollution from Ships
MLU	Ministerien für Landwirtschaft und Umwelt
MLV	Ministerium für Landesentwicklung und Verkehr
MMPA	Marine Mammal Protection Act
MMPR	Marine Mammal Protection Regulations
MPA	Marine protected area
MWA	Ministerium für Wirtschaft und Arbeit
NBV	Nordseebäderverband Schleswig-Holstein e.V.
NGO	Non-Governmental Organisation
NPG	Gesetz zum Schutz des schleswig-holsteinischen Wattenmeeres (Nationalparkgesetz)
NSF	Natural Science Fund
NTB	Nusa Tenggara Barat
NZAid	New Zealand Agency for International Development
NZCPS	New Zealand Coastal Policy Statement
NZODA	New Zealand Official Development Assistance
NZTB	New Zealand Tourism Board
PAR	Participatory Action Research
PKA	Forest Protection and Nature Conservation
PNA	Natural protected areas
PRA	Participatory Rural Appraisal
R&D	Research & Development
RISPO	Research on Innovative and Strategic Policy Options
RMA	Resource Management Act
RTMB	Rinjani Trek Management Board
RWTH	Rheinisch-Westfälische Technische Hochschule Aachen

SAM	Social Accounting Matrices
SARS	Severe Acute Respiratory Syndrome
SECTUR	Secretaría de Turismo
SÖM	Sozio-ökonomisches Monitoring
SW	SmartWood Program
TMAP	Trilaterale Wattenmeer-Monitoring
TMG	Tourismus-Marketing Sachsen-Anhalt GmbH
UAEM	Universidad Autónoma del Estado de México
UNAM	Universidad Nacional Autónoma de México
UNESCO	United Nations Educational, Scientific and Cultural Organization
UNWTO	World Tourism Organization
VDN	Verband Deutscher Naturparke e.V.
WCED	World Commission on Environment and Development
WCPA	World Commision on Protected Areas
WiSA	Wirtschaftsförderungsgesellschaft für das Land Sachsen-Anhalt mbH
WSTCF	Water Sector Technical Co-operation Fund
WTTC	World Travel and Tourism Council
WWF	World Wide Fund For Nature

Autorenverzeichnis

Dr. Wolfgang Georg Arlt, *professor and study program director at the International Tourism Management Programme (Bachelor and Master) at the FH Westküste (West Coast University of Applied Sciences) in Heide/Germany. Director of the COTRI China Outbound Tourism Research Institute. Visiting Professor of Ningbo University (China) and University of Sunderland (UK). Research Fellow of the JSPS Japanese Society for the Promotion of Science. Author and Editor of a number of publications on tourism in and out of East Asia. Contact: arlt@fh-westkueste.de.*

Maren Babinsky, *seit 2005 Studentin der Landschaftsplanung an der Technischen Universität Berlin. Zurzeit tätig im Hauptstudienprojekt „Klimafunktion von Auenböden" an der TU Berlin.*

Dipl.-Kffr. (FH) Ellen Böhling, M.A., *Studium International Tourism Management (Master of Arts), BWL-Studium (Dipl.-Kffr. FH), von 2004 bis 2006 wissenschaftliche Mitarbeiterin im Studiengang International Tourism Management an der FH Westküste, von 2006 bis 2008 Projekttätigkeit als wissenschaftliche Mitarbeiterin im Institut für Management und Tourismus (IMT). Verantwortlich für die Organisation der 1st International Tourism Conference an der FH Westküste im Jahr 2007. Seit April 2008 selbstständig in Argentinien (IMT GmbH Salta i.G.).*

Dr. Christiane Gätje, *studied biology in Berlin and Hamburg, and environmental economics in Lueneburg. She worked and teached for nine years at the botanical institute of the university in Hamburg. In 1991, she finished her doctoral study on microphytobenthos of the Elbe estuary. After three months employment at the Bundesamt für Seeschifffahrt und Hydrographie (Federal Maritime and Hydrographic Agency), she is working in the National Park authority for the Schleswig-Holstein Wadden Sea since 1992, currently being responsible for socio-economic monitoring, sustainable tourism and tourism cooperation in the National Park region.*

Dr. Fleur Fallon, *completed her doctoral studies in the Faculty of Economics, Business and Law at the University of New England, Australia in 2002. Her thesis title is: Tourism Interrupted: The challenge of sustainability for Lombok island, Indonesia 1987-2001. She has extensive experience in Human Resource Management in Australia and teaching HRM and International Business related subjects to postgraduate level in China and in Europe. Contact: fleur2@asia.com.*

Dr. Michael Lück, *currently holds the position of Associate Professor in the School of Hospitality and Tourism, AUT University in Auckland, New Zealand. He is an Associate Director of the New Zealand Tourism Research Institute (NZTRI), where he is responsible for the marine tourism research programme area. Michael's research interests are in the wider area of marine tourism, with a focus on marine wildlife tourism and interpretation and education. He is also interested in ecotourism, sustainable tourism, the impacts of tourism, aviation, and gay tourism. Michael has developed a keen interest in innovative and alternative teaching and as-*

181

sessment methods. He has published in international academic journals, and contributed to various books. He is the overall editor of four books, the Encyclopedia of Tourism and Recreation in Marine Environments (CABI), the founding editor of the academic journal Tourism in Marine Environments, and Associate Editor of the Journal of Ecotourism.

Mtro. Oscar Mario Ibarra Martínez, *has published the book "Statistics for the Tourist Administration". He presently holds the position of Academic Coordinator and has given classes for 32 years in the Tourism School of the Anahuac University. He offers a Masters Studies course in Management of Tourist Companies at the Anahuac University.*

Dipl.-Ing. Anja Maschewski *ist seit 2005 am Institut für Management und Tourismus der Fachhochschule Westküste in Heide beschäftigt und leitet dort das Kompetenzfeld „Kultur- und Naturtourismus". Als ausgebildete Landschaftsplanerin mit langjähriger praktischer Erfahrung im Tourismus- und Regionalmanagement interessieren sie insbesondere die Optimierungspotenziale zur nachhaltigen Entwicklung touristischer Regionen. Anja Maschewski hat im Bereich Biodiversität und Tourismus veröffentlicht, an der Vorbereitung der Charta für Nachhaltigen Tourismus mitgewirkt und sich in zahlreichen Studien mit den Auswirkungen touristischer Nutzungen auf Natur- und Landschaftsräume beschäftigt. Ihr gegenwärtiger Forschungsschwerpunkt ist die Strategische Steuerung von Kultur- und Freizeiteinrichtungen zur nachhaltigen Sicherung kulturtouristischer Infrastruktur in ländlich geprägten Räumen. Anja Maschewski unterrichtet zudem Destinationsmanagement an der Fachhochschule Westküste.*

Diplom Kaufmann (FH) Matthias Poeschel, *seit 2004 ist Matthias Poeschel als Projektmanager in der touristischen Vermarktung des Landes Sachsen-Anhalt tätig. Das von ihm koordinierte Projekt „Naturreich Sachsen-Anhalt" erzielt 2006 deutschlandweit große Beachtung. Intensive Erfahrungen im Management von Großschutzgebieten sammelte er bereits von 1999 bis 2003 in Uganda und Ecuador. Seine Aufgabenschwerpunkte im Tourismus sieht Matthias Poeschel in der Verknüpfung von soziokulturellen, ökonomischen sowie ökologischen Aspekten und in der Netzwerkbildung von touristischen und tourismusaffinen Partnern.*

Mtro. Alexander Oliver Scherer Leibold, *is currently the coordinator of the Bachelor of Gastronomy and of the Service Area and Tourism Enterprise for the School of Tourism. He is also coordinator of professional practice and representative for Social Activities at the University. He completed a master's degree in marketing and publicity.*

Dipl.-Geogr. Manuel Woltering, *The author studied economic geography at the Ludwig-Maximilians-Universität München and does currently his doctorate at the Julius-Maximilians-Universität Würzburg advised by Prof. Dr. Hubert Job. His research is focused on tourism and its regional economic impacts, especially in protected areas.*

Dr. Xu Honggang, *Professor, associate dean of The school of Tourism Management, Sun Yat-sen University. Her research interests are in the complexity of the tourism system, tourism planning and sustainable tourism. She has also participated as a deputy team leader in the important tourism planning projects by Chinese Tourism Administration, Hunan Provincial Governments, etc. She was also invited to be the guest professors in Angers University, Asian Institute of Technology and researcher in Rikkyo University, Tokyo.*

Institut für Management und Tourismus der FH Westküste

Das Institut für Management und Tourismus (IMT) ist seit Juni 2006 als In-Institut an der Fachhochschule Westküste angesiedelt. Unter dem Dach des Instituts werden sämtliche Hochschulaktivitäten in den Feldern betriebswirtschaftlich orientierter Tourismusforschung, -qualifizierung und -beratung gebündelt und miteinander vernetzt. Großer Wert wird dabei auf Unabhängigkeit der Forschung, Nähe zur Praxis und wissenschaftliche Fundierung gelegt.

Das IMT entstand im Rahmen des Projektes „Aufbau eines Kompetenzzentrums für betriebswirtschaftliche Tourismusforschung und -qualifizierung". Gefördert wird dieses Projekt aus Mitteln des Europäischen Sozialfonds und des Innovationsfonds Schleswig-Holstein. Weitere Unterstützung erfährt das Kompetenzzentrum durch finanzielle Zuschüsse weiterer Partner und durch einen Projektbeirat mit Akteuren aus Wirtschaft, Wissenschaft und Politik.

Das Kompetenzzentrum verfolgt als zentraler Bestandteil des Bildungs-, Beratungs- und Forschungsschwerpunktes Tourismus der Fachhochschule Westküste die Zielsetzung, die wissenschaftliche Weiterbildung und Qualifizierung im Tourismus zu fördern sowie u. a. über anwendungsorientierte Forschungsprojekte den Wissenstransfer zwischen Hochschule und Wirtschaft zu intensivieren.

 Die Schriftenreihe des IMT wird im Rahmen des Projektes „Aufbau eines Kompetenzzentrums für betriebswirtschaftliche Tourismusforschung und -qualifizierung" aus Mitteln des Europäischen Sozialfonds gefördert.

Einen besonderen Dank für ihre Unterstützung bei der Erstellung dieses Bandes richten die Herausgeber an Frau Ellen Böhling, Frau Ciara Colgan-Buchenau und Frau Dörte Renken.

Schriftenreihe des Instituts für Management und Tourismus:

Besucherleitsysteme

Entwicklung und Anwendung eines Instruments zu ihrer Bewertung –
Dargestellt am Beispiel des Biosphärenreservats Rhön
(Schriftenreihe des Instituts für Management und Tourismus 1)
Von Christian Eilzer
2007, 197 Seiten, Paperback, Euro 29,90/CHF 51,00, ISBN 978-3-89975-095-9

Besucherleitsysteme sind wichtige Bestandteile der Angebotspalette einer
Destination. Für Touristen sind Informationspunkte, Wander- oder Hotelleitsys-
teme bedeutsame Orientierungshilfen, die unter anderem zur Erhöhung der
Angebotsqualität beitragen.
In dieser Arbeit wird eine Methodik zur Bewertung und Optimierung von Leit-
einrichtungen entwickelt und auf das Biosphärenreservat Rhön angewendet.

Qualität und Qualifizierung im Tourismus

Anforderungen an ein ganzheitliches Qualitäts- und
Qualifizierungssystem in einer Destination
(Schriftenreihe des Instituts für Management und Tourismus 2)
Von Manon Eckhoff
2007, 166 Seiten, Paperback, Euro 29,90/CHF 53,50, ISBN 978-3-89975-111-6

Die Betonung der Qualität – insbesondere in der Dienstleistung – ist für Destinationen ein zentraler Erfolgsfaktor im touristischen Wettbewerb. Damit
steigen auch die Ansprüche an die Qualifikation der Akteure.
In dieser Arbeit werden die Anforderungen an ein ganzheitliches Qualitäts- und
Qualifizierungssystem für Destinationen abgeleitet und konzeptionelle Leitlinien für die Entwicklung eines Systems zur Optimierung der touristischen
Angebotsqualität formuliert.

Ihr Wissenschaftsverlag. Kompetent und unabhängig.

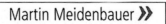

Martin Meidenbauer »

Verlagsbuchhandlung GmbH & Co. KG
Erhardtstr. 8 • 80469 München
Tel. (089) 20 23 86 -03 • Fax -04
info@m-verlag.net • www.m-verlag.net